BRISTOL
PLAQUES

BRISTOL PLAQUES

MAURICE FELLS

The
History
Press

First published 2016

The History Press
The Mill, Brimscombe Port
Stroud, Gloucestershire, GL5 2QG
www.thehistorypress.co.uk

British Library Cataloguing in Publication Data.
A catalogue record for this book is available from the British Library.

ISBN 978 0 7509 6531 6

Typesetting and origination by The History Press
Printed and bound by CPI Group (UK) Ltd

CONTENTS

ACKNOWLEDGEMENTS

As a passionate Bristolian with a deep love for the city's long and colourful history, researching and writing this book has truly been a labour of love, especially when I discovered some notable people whom I didn't know had strong links with this city.

This book is the result of delving into a combination of resources including old newspapers and magazines and my own archive of press releases, brochures and other publicity material that I have built up whilst working as a journalist on newspapers, radio and television.

Early editions of the *Western Daily Press*, founded in the middle of the nineteenth century, and the *Bristol Evening Post*, which first rolled off the presses in 1932, proved to be extremely helpful in providing details of citizens whose names are rarely, if at all, mentioned these days. Another source was the inscriptions, many of them weather-beaten, on the plaques themselves. Some were more informative than others. I turned to *Chambers Biographical Dictionary* to discover missing birth, death and other anniversary dates.

I made many visits to Bristol Central Library where the staff were most patient and courteous in dealing with my many questions. I must especially thank Dawn Dyer of the reference section for her enthusiasm in my book and for searching out files that were many, many years old and probably rarely looked at.

Thanks must also go to the various local history and amenity groups for their immense help. Maggie Shapland of Clifton and Hotwells Improvement Society was always happy to pass on information, as was Pauline Luscombe of the Barton Hill History Group. The group's publication *Cotton Thread* by Gary Atterton, one of its members, was extremely helpful. Simon Birch of Bristol Civic Society has to be thanked for explaining how the society would be running the Bristol Blue Plaque scheme which it had taken over from Bristol City Council, even before it had been publicly announced.

The slim but important publication *100 Bristol Women* by Shirley Brown was an excellent source of information.

I must apologise to the artist extraordinaire, Mike Baker, designer of so many unusual and colourful plaques which bring the history of the Easton and Barton Hill districts to life for the numerous times I dragged him away from his studio to answer my queries. Andrew Ward of Wards of Bristol was extremely helpful in explaining the process of making plaques and the history of his firm.

This book would never have been published without the immense help and encouragement of Nicola Guy of The History Press who along with her team of editors and designer Chris West has turned my typed manuscript into a wonderful publication.

Last but certainly not least, Janet and Trevor Naylor deserve a big round of thanks for patiently and meticulously checking the manuscript before it was sent to the publishers. Trevor also spent much time treading the pavements and even the river banks of Bristol searching for plaques to photograph. The result of his many treks around town can be seen in the photographs that help to bring this book to life.

All images are courtesy of Trevor Naylor, with the following exceptions: page 30 (author's collection), page 33 (courtesy of Clifton College) and page 112 (courtesy of the Bristol Civic Society).

INTRODUCTION

Researching this book has involved spending a lot of time strolling the streets of Bristol looking for signs of the dead. It seems that at every turn, from cul-de-sacs to crescents, from side streets to Georgian squares and from parades to promenades you will find a plaque. Many of them are mounted on walls of homes, businesses and pubs although some are set in the pavement and one is even embedded in concrete on a riverbank. Bristol not only has the traditional blue plaques; there are also bronze, green, black, red and even multi-coloured ones and they come in all sorts of shapes and sizes. There's no doubt about it, Bristol offers anyone who is interested in the city's history a feast of plaques.

It's not just eminent scientists, statesmen, politicians, artists, explorers and high-flying aircraft designers and engineers who have been honoured with a commemorative plaque. There is also the toilet attendant who befriended prostitutes, the woman who hoaxed villagers into believing that she was a princess, and the schoolboy cricketer who's score of 628 not out was a world record for 116 years. And there's the former prisoner whose book was turned into a top West End musical.

Bristol has so many plaques largely because the city has been associated with so many important national and even international events. The Italian explorer John Cabot sailed from the city's harbour and according to a bronze memorial tablet in the city centre discovered 'the continent of North

America'. Thomas Clarkson visited Bristol to gather information about the slave trade with which the city was heavily involved. The evidence he gathered helped to bring about the abolition of the trade. Bristol-born Elizabeth Blackwell was the first woman in modern times to qualify as a doctor, albeit in America, and another native of the city, the publisher John Cottle, helped to give birth to the Romantic movement in English poetry. Alexander Selkirk, a marooned sailor thought to be the inspiration for Daniel Defoe's novel *Robinson Crusoe*, is said to have met the author at a dockside tavern. And, of course, there was Isambard Kingdom Brunel, the great Victorian engineer who transformed the face of the city with his bridges, a railway system and a hotel. These and many other historic events have each given rise to a plaque.

But it's not just people who are featured on plaques in Bristol. A traditional blue one has been dedicated to Nipper, a Jack Russell terrier, who became an international trademark.

The idea of placing commemorative plaques on the homes of the great and the good was conceived by William Ewart, a Liberal Member of Parliament. He put his idea to the House of Commons in 1863, which gave it immediate support. The idea was taken up by the Society of Arts (now Royal Society of Arts) but since 1986 English Heritage has run the traditional blue plaque scheme.

The first blue plaque was erected in 1867 and marked Lord Bryon's birthplace in Cavendish Square, London. However, the oldest surviving blue plaque in the country is believed to be one which in 1867 was fixed on a house in St James, London, where Napoleon III once lived.

Many other similar blue plaque schemes, usually run by local authorities, have come into operation all over the country. Bristol City Council administered the scheme across the city from the 1960s until 2015 but it is now run by the long-established Bristol Civic Society. Its blue plaques panel has drawn up a set of basic ground rules under which the scheme operates. Nobody can be nominated, for example, until at least a year has passed since their death, to allow for a more objective assessment of their contribution. Advertising is not permitted and the panel must approve the design and wording.

The Civic Society does not itself nominate people for plaques, and neither does it have a budget for them. The person or group nominating someone to be honoured has to raise the funding themselves. They must also provide evidence that the person being nominated had a connection with the site being recommended for the plaque. The permission of the site owner has to be obtained and the case for the nominee's commemoration must be put to the Civic Society. The society says:

> We want to take advantage of people's enthusiasm for blue plaques by encouraging Bristolians to come forward and nominate men and women connected with the city who have made an impact. They do not have to be national figures. We are just as interested in those who worked tirelessly for their own communities. And they don't have to be people from the distant past. It is just as important to honour more recent figures, so that the scheme can also reflect Bristol as it is today.

The society's first plaque honours three sisters, Berta Sacof, Helen Bloom and Jeannette Britton, for their 'service to the community'. All sisters were members of Bristol City Council and Helen Bloom was also Lord Mayor in 1971. Although Bristol has had mayors, later Lord Mayors, since 1216 Helen Bloom was only the third woman to be elected by her fellow councillors to hold the prestigious office.

Other plaque schemes in Bristol are restricted to specific geographical areas or celebrate a particular theme. It seems that the suburb of Clifton led the way with the Clifton Improvement Committee, founded in 1900, installing impressive bronze plaques on the former homes of famous people. Many of these plaques are now as historic as the people they commemorate. Many of them are still in position although the Clifton Improvement Committee no longer exists.

Clifton and Hotwells Improvement Society, founded in 1968, and one of the largest amenity groups in the country with more than 1,100 members, has taken over the task of perpetuating the memories of the famous. Its green circular plaques are a familiar sight around the two districts in which it takes an interest.

In the Barton Hill and Easton districts local history groups remember not only well-known people from their communities but also historic buildings that have long fallen into the mouth of the bulldozer in the name of progress.

Mike Baker, a local artist and historian with a heritage degree, designs many of the Barton Hill and Easton plaques. His multi-coloured, bas-relief and interpretative three-dimensional style plaques tell a story and draw people in as well as bringing the history of the district to life. They are cast in both bronze and aluminium, many of them by Wards of Bristol, a family-run business which has more than half a century of sign-making tradition. A growing demand for plaques, both traditional and modern, from all over the country has helped to keep the firm in business.

In 2006, to coincide with the bicentenary of Isambard Kingdom Brunel's birth, the Retired Professional Engineers' Club inaugurated an 'engineering wall of fame' on the outside wall of Bristol Aquarium. Its blue plaques celebrate the work of great engineers and scientists who have been involved with shipping, roads and bridges, the aircraft industry, railways and the brass industry. All those honoured by a plaque have local connections.

The size of most plaques prohibits much information being given about the person or event being commemorated save for the barest of details. Writers of history books and guidebooks to Bristol make casual references to some of the city's plaques but rarely tell the tale behind the name on the wall.

This book, the first of its kind in Bristol, aims to fill that fascinating gap. It not only provides potted biographies of many remarkable men and women but also puts the spotlight on their connection with the city and provides the locations of plaques. However, it does not set out to be a definitive guide to every plaque in Bristol for the simple reason that no one knows exactly how many there are. Unfortunately, there is not a comprehensive list of plaques provided by the various organisations. So, I may well have missed some, especially if they are now obscured by overgrown shrubbery or trees. But more than likely, the ever active local history organisations and amenity groups have probably put up some more plaques in the time between my completing the manuscript of this book and its publication.

Bristol Plaques acknowledges the achievements of remarkable people, some of whom may otherwise have gone unsung.

Maurice Fells, 2016

1

PERSONAL PLAQUES

REVD CANON ALFRED AINGER (1837-1904)
WRITER AND CHURCH OF ENGLAND CLERGYMAN
PLAQUE: CLIFTON ROAD, BS8 1BS

When he was appointed a canon of Bristol Cathedral in 1887 the Revd Alfred Ainger found that apart from the usual religious services there were no other activities taking place in the church. It was not long before he introduced a number of lectures on literary subjects, readings from Shakespeare and other dramatic productions. The move seems to have been popular with the rest of the cathedral clergy and the congregation because after his death a memorial window was installed in honour of Canon Ainger. Mr Ainger also preached at neighbouring churches and taught at the cathedral school.

During his clerical career Mr Ainger held various prestigious posts including those of Assistant Master of the Collegiate School, Sheffield; Master of the Temple in London's legal enclave, off The Strand; and Chaplain in Ordinary to both Queen Victoria and Edward VII.

While he was at Bristol Cathedral Mr Ainger was noted for making it almost a duty to climb the steep hills to his home in Clifton each day. Apparently, he refused offers of transport until poor health forced him to do so.

As residentiary canon of the cathedral he was required to live in the city for three months a year. As there wasn't any cathedral property available for his accommodation Mr Ainger rented Richmond House, a handsome early eighteenth-century mansion on Clifton Road overlooking the much better known Palladian-style Clifton Hill House. However, a small black plaque on one side of the front door of Richmond House states that it is 'an English Listed Building'.

Another plaque on the front of the house commemorates the Reverend Ainger. Its inscription says that Mr Ainger 'Master of the Temple, friend of Dickens, and biographer of the essayist Charles Lamb lived here 1888–1898'. Apart from writing a life of the essayist Lamb, he contributed to biographies on some of the 'literary greats' of the day, including Alfred Tennyson, to the *Dictionary of National Biography*. These entries were always published under the initials 'A.A.'.

Ainger's friendship with Dickens went back to the days when he attended school with two of the authors' sons, and sometimes was invited to their home.

THOMAS BEDDOES (1760-1808)

SCIENTIST AND PHYSICIAN

PLAQUES:
RODNEY PLACE, CLIFTON, BS8 4HY
11 HOPE SQUARE, BS8 4LX
6 DOWRY SQUARE, BS8 4SH

Dr Thomas Beddoes had a traditional education at Oxford University, where he later became a reader in Chemistry, but when he set up his medical practice in Bristol he became known as the doctor with 'curious cures'.

He set up a laboratory in a Georgian house in Hope Square, Hotwells, but wasn't there long before he opened what he grandly called his Pneumatic Institute at nearby Dowry Square. A local newspaper reported that Dr Beddoes could treat 'incurable diseases including consumption, dropsy and obstinate venereal complaints'.

One of his ideas was to cure or prevent consumption by the inhalation of gases, and amongst other experiments extensive trials with nitrous oxide, also known as laughing gas, were carried out at the institute. Dr Beddoes also recommended that his patients should enjoy the company of cows and inhale the gases they exhaled from both ends of their body. He even drove milking cows upstairs into patients' bedrooms and used oil stoves to raise the room temperature even higher. One of his patients was reported as claiming that she slept three nights in a cow shed and was cured of her illness.

It was said that Dr Beddoes also tried to bleach the skin of a black man white by making him hold his arm in a jar of oxide gas. Needless to say this experiment was in vain.

To help him run his institute Dr Beddoes employed a 19-year-old man from Penzance, Humphrey Davy, who had been recommended to him as a 'clever chemist and promising young man'. Beddoes appointed Davy as superintendent of the institute and also provided him with accommodation at his home in Clifton.

Beddoes ran the institute for about three years and when Davy left he turned it into a charitable dispensary, called the Preventive Medicine Institute for the Sick and Drooping Poor. Beddoes died at his home aged 48, suffering from dropsy in the chest.

A large black plaque, erected by the long-defunct Clifton Improvement Board, is attached to Dr Beddoes' house in Rodney Place, Clifton. The inscription states that his son, Thomas Lovell Beddoes, who became a poet and physiologist, was born there in 1803. While he was still at school he wrote a drama called *The Bride's Tragedy*. After he died at the age of 46, a friend published *Poems by the late Thomas Lovell Beddoes*.

The rather informative tablet at his birthplace also tells us that one of the visitors to the house was Maria Edgeworth, an aunt of the young Beddoes. She was a novelist, who also wrote books on education as well as improving stories for children. There is also a plaque, erected by Clifton and Hotwells Improvement Society, outside a house in Hope Square which simply reads 'Thomas Beddoes, scientist, worked here 1793–99'. There is also a plaque outside Dr Beddoes' Institute at Dowry Square.

ERNEST BEVIN (1881-1951)

TRADE UNION LEADER AND POLITICIAN

PLAQUE: 39 SAXON ROAD, BS2 9 UQ

The life story of Ernest Bevin could be summed up in the sort of front-page headline that editors of tabloid newspapers love: 'From van boy to Cabinet Minister'.

Bevin was born in the Somerset village of Winsford, in the heart of Exmoor, as far away as one could imagine from the corridors of power in Westminster and Whitehall. His formal education, for what it was, ended when he was only 11 years old and Bevin was sent to work on a farm. Two years later he found himself working as a kitchen boy in a restaurant in the centre of Bristol. Later Bevin became a van boy and subsequently drove a van delivering bottles of mineral water for a local firm.

He soon took an interest in local politics and was appointed unpaid secretary of the Bristol Right-to-Work Committee. Bevin was later involved with the merger of fourteen trades unions and 300,000 workers to form the mighty Transport and General Workers' Union, which was officially launched on New Year's Day 1922. He became the union's general secretary, a post he held for nearly twenty years.

After the General Strike of 1926 Ernest Bevin strengthened his links with the Labour Party and was eventually elected as a Member of Parliament. He was a Labour minister in Winston Churchill's coalition government of 1940–45 and after the Labour Party's landslide victory in 1945 he was appointed foreign secretary in Atlee's government. By the early 1950s poor health had caught up with Ernest Bevin, causing him to resign from government in March 1951. He died a month later.

Before the First World War Ernest Bevin married a wine taster's daughter and the couple made their home in Saxon Road, St Werburghs. A blue plaque honouring Ernest Bevin is fixed to the terraced house with an inscription stating that he lived there, although it does not say for how long.

ELIZABETH BLACKWELL (1821–1910)

PIONEERING PHYSICIAN

PLAQUE: 1 WILSON STREET. BS2 9HH

With her doggedness and determination Elizabeth Blackwell must have been an inspiration to all women when she achieved her goal of becoming a doctor. Indeed, she was the first British woman to become a general practitioner, albeit qualifying in America.

Initially she was refused entry to the medical colleges with their all-male students and staff who were against women joining them. Elizabeth Blackwell eventually succeeded in getting a place at Geneva Medical College, New York State. Not only did she graduate as a doctor but also came top of her class.

Elizabeth Blackwell, the third of nine daughters of a sugar refiner, was born at Counterslip, but when she was just 3 years old the family moved to Wilson Street in the St Paul's district of Bristol where she was brought up. Eight years later, with the infectious disease cholera raging in Bristol, her father took the family to America where he set up a refinery. Ironically, cholera was also rampant in New York where the Blackwell's settled.

After her father's death in 1838 Elizabeth helped to support the family financially by teaching, although she devoted much of her spare time to studying medicine using textbooks that were borrowed from friends. In 1847 she was admitted as a student to Geneva Medical College.

After qualifying Elizabeth worked in a hospital in Paris, later joining the staff of the renowned St Bartholomew's Hospital, London, before returning to New York to set up a hospital which was staffed by women only. She later returned to Britain, where she was the first woman to have her name entered on the British medical register. Unfortunately, she contracted an eye disease from a patient, losing the sight in one eye, which put an end to her ambition to be a surgeon. But that didn't prevent her working in medicine until she was in her mid eighties.

Elizabeth Blackwell is honoured for her work by a plaque mounted on the wall of her childhood home in Wilson Street, St Paul's. A plate beneath it states that the plaque was 'donated by the Medical Women's

Federation and Friends'. Appropriately, it was unveiled by the late Dr Beryl Corner, a Bristol-born physician who was the first consultant paediatrician in the south-west of England, a position that she achieved in the face of male prejudice. Dr Corner became a national pioneer in the care of newborn children.

JACK (JOHN) BOARD (1867-1924)
GLOUCESTERSHIRE AND ENGLAND CRICKETER
PLAQUE: 22 MANOR ROAD, BS7 8PY

Jack Board was wicket keeper and batsman for Gloucestershire County Cricket Club for twenty years without a break, after being picked out of the relative obscurity of club cricket by W.G. Grace. He joined the county side in 1891 and played in 525 first-class matches. As a batsman he scored a total of 15,674 runs with Gloucestershire; his highest score being 214 against Somerset at Bristol.

Jack Board was born in Clifton and by trade was a gardener.

He was picked as England wicket keeper for Test match tours of South Africa between 1899 and 1906.

He died at the age of 57 on board the *Kenilworth Castle* when he was returning home from an annual winter coaching engagement in South Africa. A blue plaque on a house in Bishopston states that Jack Board lived there from 1896 until 1902.

DOROTHY BROWN (1927-2013)
ENVIRONMENTAL CAMPAIGNER
PLAQUE: 5 BUCKINGHAM VALE, BS8 2BU

Dorothy Brown, who was born in Berwick-upon-Tweed, England's most northern town, and educated in Edinburgh, only moved to Bristol as her husband had a job in the city. Despite her northern background Dorothy came to love Bristol so much that she became an indefatigable campaigner to save its historic buildings.

Her campaigning began in earnest in 1970 when plans were revealed to build an eight-storey hotel on the rock face of the Avon Gorge close to Brunel's Clifton Suspension Bridge. She discovered that a number of her friends were also against the plans for the proposed hotel. Dorothy Brown co-ordinated a city-wide battle to fight the developers; eventually the project was turned down by the government.

She set up the Bristol Visual and Environmental Group to combat Bristol City Council's development plan of 1966 with its proposals to destroy many of the city's historic buildings. Some 400 of them were earmarked to fall into the mouth of the bulldozer but Dorothy managed to save many of them. There were also plans to fill in the city's harbour with concrete to make way for a major road scheme. Following city-wide protests by environmentalists, including Dorothy Brown, this project never came to fruition.

In 1971 she set up the Conservation Advisory Panel to advise the city council on planning matters. She served on the panel right up until her death. As part of her campaigning Dorothy also wrote books about the city's heritage and focused the spotlight on buildings in need of restoration.

In recognition of her work she was awarded an MBE in 1988. Three years later Bristol University awarded her an honorary Master of Arts degree.

Dorothy Brown died suddenly aged 86 in her local public library, where she was doing research for an exhibition that she was organising about Bristol's heritage.

In 2015 Clifton and Hotwells Improvement Society unveiled a plaque in honour of Dorothy Brown's life and campaigning work outside the house in Clifton in which she lived between 1955 and 2013. An inscription on the plaque describes her as a 'tireless campaigner'.

ISAMBARD KINGDOM BRUNEL (1806-1859)

ENGINEER

PLAQUES:
CLIFTON SUSPENSION BRIDGE. BS8 3PA
ANCHOR ROAD. BS1 5LL
GAS FERRY ROAD. BS1 6TY

The great Victorian engineer Isambard Kingdom Brunel who designed the Clifton Suspension Bridge referred to it as 'my first child, my darling'. But unfortunately he never saw the bridge, which airily spans the Avon Gorge 245ft above the River Avon, finished. He died five years before the first pedestrian and horse and cart crossed it when it opened in 1864. An inscription on a plaque fixed to the pier at the Clifton end of the bridge says it was completed as a 'monument to Brunel'.

Another plaque on the pier was unveiled in 1986 to mark the 150th anniversary of the laying of the bridge's foundation stone by the Marquess of Northampton. This ceremony took place on the 27 August 1836 at 7.15 a.m. Afterwards Brunel, along with a party of invited guests, enjoyed a celebratory breakfast.

Clifton Suspension Bridge.

Construction work on the bridge started in 1831 but was dogged by financial problems. Just seven years later work was brought to a halt when the contractors went bankrupt. Another firm took over but in 1843 funds ran out and work temporarily stopped again. In all, it took thirty-three years to build the bridge.

Brunel came to Bristol to recover from an accident whilst working for his father on the Rotherhithe Tunnel under the River Thames. While convalescing he entered a competition to design a bridge that would cross the Avon Gorge, linking Clifton on the Bristol side with Leigh Woods on the Somerset side. The judging panel eventually accepted a design by Brunel as the winning entry. He initially planned to build giant sphinxes – a fashionable decoration at the time – on the top of the bridge's two piers but this proved to be financially prohibitive.

Brunel was not a man who let the grass grow under his feet. Whilst working on the bridge he accepted the job of engineer to the Great Western Railway. He masterminded construction of its network of many hundreds of miles of track, its tunnels, viaducts and bridges. Brunel was also responsible for some of the modifications to Bristol's Floating Harbour. In a busy life he also built ships, advised on the construction of railways as far away as Australia and East Bengal, and even designed a military hospital for use in the Crimean War.

To coincide with the bicentenary of Brunel's birth in 2006 the Retired Professional Engineers' Club of Bristol set up an engineering 'wall of fame' in the centre of the city known as Engineers' Walk. It consists of blue plaques on a wall in Anchor Road honouring great engineers and scientists with local connections. The inscription on the one dedicated to Brunel includes a list of some of the many projects with which he was involved.

Another plaque dedicated to Brunel is at the entrance to the Great Western Dockyard in Gas Ferry Road, where the restored SS *Great Britain* has become a nationally renowned tourist attraction. Donated by the Transport Trust, this large red circular plaque pays tribute to Brunel and the SS *Great Britain*, which he designed. The dedication states that the ship was 'launched here in 1843 as the world's largest and the first iron-hulled, screw propelled ocean going ship'. The SS *Great Britain*, in the shape of a rusting hulk, was towed on a pontoon back to Bristol in 1970 from the Falkland Islands where she had been scuttled for many years.

WILLIAM BUDD (1811-1880)

PHYSICIAN AND EPIDEMIOLOGIST

PLAQUES:
89 PARK STREET, BS1 5PW
13 LANSDOWN PLACE, BS8 3AF

Dr William Budd, who was one of the country's most outstanding contributors to medical science, earned the nickname The Father of Health through his campaigning for clean water. He was the pioneer of the preventative medicine that made Bristol healthy.

While he was physician at the Bristol Infirmary Dr Budd was looking after patients suffering from typhoid, cholera and typhus. Having survived typhoid fever himself and seen the insanitary slum conditions in which people lived, Dr Budd became passionate about improving the city's sanitary system.

He became one of the first directors of the Bristol Waterworks Company when it was formed in 1846. The company was later responsible for water supplies across the city, making obsolete the many local systems of supply which had operated for centuries.

Dr Budd gave evidence to the 1854 Royal Commission on health in towns, which marked Bristol down as being the third unhealthiest place in the United Kingdom. He recognised the need for disinfection and prevention of sewage entering the water supply and set about improving water supplies. When the cholera epidemic of 1866 reached Bristol, death figures were far lower than in an epidemic twenty years earlier. This was put down to Dr Budd's work.

When the British Medical Association met in Bristol in 1863 he was chosen to give the address to the delegates on medicine. He spoke for more than an hour, stressing the fact that contagious diseases were due to living organisms – something he had proved during a widespread epidemic among sheep.

One of his most valuable works was considered to be his book *Typhoid Fever*, published in 1873. Dr Budd was the first to show that this disease was contagious.

William Budd, who was the son of a doctor in Devon, trained in London, Paris and Edinburgh, where he was awarded his medical degree. In Bristol, besides working at the infirmary, he was also a physician at the old St Peter's Hospital. He also lectured at the Bristol Medical School – believed to be the first such institution to be formed in England. Dr Budd also set up his own medical practice.

He died aged 80 and is commemorated by two plaques in Bristol. One, on the wall of a restaurant on Park Street, states that Dr Budd lived in a house on the site from 1853–55. The other, erected by Clifton and Hotwells Improvement Society, is fixed to a house in Lansdown Place, Clifton, where he lived from 1860–65.

DAME CLARA BUTT (1872-1936)

INTERNATIONAL SINGER

PLAQUE: 3 BELLE VUE, TOTTERDOWN, BS4 2BG

The conductor Sir Thomas Beecham swore that the booming contralto voice of Bristol's best-known concert recitalist and singer could be heard as far away as Calais on the French side of the English Channel. Apparently, Dame Clara Butt inherited her voice, with its remarkable range and power, from her mother.

Clara Butt was born in West Sussex but when she was about 9 years old her family moved to Bristol and found a home in Totterdown. A blue plaque on a house in Belle Vue records that she lived there from 1882–86.

After taking singing lessons at a local school Clara was performing in concerts in church halls and joined the Bristol Festival Chorus. She was so popular that Bristolians raised enough money for her to be trained at the Royal College of Music in London. It's said that at her audition the examiners sat up when Clara, who was an imposing 6ft 2in tall, boomed out a song called 'The Enchantress'. She was asked to sing something quieter. Nonetheless, the college accepted her.

After making her professional debut at the Royal Albert Hall, singing in an opera at 19 years old, Clara became hugely famous and very wealthy. The composer Edward Elgar wrote his song cycle *Sea Pictures* especially for her. She was often asked to sing privately for Queen Victoria at Windsor

Castle. The queen is reputed to have said: 'I have never liked the English language before but in your mouth it is beautiful.'

Although she sang in concerts all over the world Clara never forgot Bristol, often returning to sing at the Colston Hall. When she married baritone Kennerley Rumford in 1900, she turned down the chance to have her wedding in St Paul's Cathedral. She said she wanted to be married in the city that had put her on the path to fame. The ceremony took place at Bristol Cathedral on 26 June 1900. There was so much interest that shops, offices and factories closed for half a day so that staff could see the wedding. Special trains ran from London to Bristol on the day.

One newspaper reported that the cathedral 'was full to suffocation' and that 'thousands of people were left outside vainly clamouring for admission'. As a wedding gift the people of Bristol bought the singer a diamond and ruby brooch formed by the initials 'C.B.' transfixed by a ruby arrow. The initials stood for either those of her name or those of the city of Bristol.

Clara Butt was made a dame in 1920 in recognition of the many thousands of pounds she had raised for the Red Cross at her concerts during the First World War. She died when she was 63 years old, suffering from spinal cancer, two years after what turned out to be her final concert at Sydney, Australia, in 1934.

JOHN (C. 1450–C. 1500) AND SEBASTIAN CABOT (1477–1557)

EXPLORERS

PLAQUES:
QUAY HEAD, BS1 1EB
ST NICHOLAS STREET, BS1 1UA
BRANDON HILL PARK

A trail of bronze plaques set in concrete was unveiled at Quay Head in the centre of Bristol in 1932 by the Premier of Nova Scotia to mark various chapters from the city's maritime history. One of them commemorates the epic voyage that the explorer Giovanni Caboto, better known as John Cabot, and his son Sebastian, who was born in Bristol, made from the city in 1497. With a crew of eighteen local men they left the harbour in their

The replica of *The Matthew* in the Avon Gorge.

50-ton wooden caravel, *The Matthew,* hoping to discover trading routes with Asia.

The plaque records, however, that once across the Atlantic Ocean John Cabot and his crew made landfall on 24 June 1497 at Cape North having, says the inscription, 'discovered the continent of America'. It is believed that Cabot and a small party went ashore and claimed the land for the King of England.

When Cabot, who was born in Genoa, returned to Bristol on 6 August 1497 he was welcomed by the sound of bells ringing out from the many church towers around the harbour. He went to London to meet King Henry VII who had granted him a patent to 'seeke out, discover and finde new land for England'. The king gave him a pension of £20 along with his gratitude.

The following May Cabot left Bristol on another voyage, this time with five ships and 300 men, but there is no further trace of him. It is assumed that he lost his life at sea. Sebastian Cabot later went to Spain and was appointed a cartographer to Ferdinand. He returned to England in 1547 and was made Grand Pilot of England.

Another plaque relating to Cabot — this one showing its age with bits peeling off — can be found on the side wall of the old St Nicholas church, in St Nicholas Street, in the centre of the city. It simply says that 'John Cabot navigator and venturer lived on this street'.

A replica of *The Matthew* was built in Redcliffe Wharf as part of the celebrations to mark the 500th anniversary of Cabot's voyage. When it was completed *The Matthew* recreated Cabot's voyage and on 24 June 1997 the little ship was welcomed into the port at Bona Vista, Newfoundland, by Queen Elizabeth II. *The Matthew* is now moored in Bristol's harbour and has become a major tourist attraction.

On the 400th anniversary of Cabot's voyage Bristolians built a 105ft tower of red sandstone and Bath freestone on Brandon Hill park in the centre of the city. At the base of the tower is a bronze plaque which states that 'the foundation stone of this tower was laid by the Marquis of Dufferin and Ava, on 24 June 1897'.

According to the plaque, a little over a year later the former Governor General of Canada was back in Bristol to officially open the tower with its viewing balcony at the top.

The plaque is of unknown origin although two names can be found at the bottom — a Mr Arrowsmith and a Mr Clarke, who are described as 'the executive committee'.

DON CAMERON (1939–)

BALLOON PILOT AND MANUFACTURER

PLAQUE: ENGINEERS' WALK, ANCHOR ROAD, BS1 5LL

Aeronautical engineer Don Cameron gave up a career in the aircraft industry to set up a business making hot-air balloons. He began making balloons as a hobby in the basement of his home in Bristol before moving into a nearby church hall. He eventually gave up his full-time job and now runs the world's largest balloon factory in an old printing and packaging works across the city.

Don's firm designs and makes balloons used for pleasure flights or competitive flying and has developed the technology to produce its world-famous special shapes including a *Fantasia* castle for Disney; a bust of Beethoven; an Orient Express train; golf balls; bottles and cans of beer; Mickey Mouse and, of course, Donald Duck.

Cameron's firm has also made the high altitude long-distance balloons used for the world record-breaking flights by Sir Richard Branson, Brian Jones and Andy Elson.

Don's love for ballooning started in 1967 when, along with some friends, he built the first modern hot-air balloon in Western Europe, which he named the *Bristol Belle*. It was made of red and white striped sailcloth and soared into the sky for the first time from an airfield in Oxfordshire.

With the help of the Bristol Junior Chamber of Commerce Don created the first Bristol Balloon fiesta in 1979 at Ashton Court estate on the southern edge of Bristol with just twenty-seven balloonists taking part. Since then it has become an annual three-day event attracting up to 150 balloonists from around the world.

Don Cameron holds many ballooning records himself and has been awarded gold, silver and bronze medals by the British Royal Aero Club for his achievements. His many honours include America's Harman Trophy presented to him at the White House, an award previously held by Charles Lindbergh and Neil Armstrong. Unfortunately, Cameron's attempt to make the first Atlantic crossing by balloon in 1978 came to an end when bad weather brought his craft down in sight of the French coast after flying 2,000 miles. He was, however, the first person to cross the Sahara Desert by hot air balloon.

His success has been recognised by members of the Retired Professional Engineers' Club who have honoured him with a blue plaque on their wall of engineering fame in Anchor Road. The plaque lists some of his many achievements, both in the air and on the ground, making balloons.

'PRINCESS CARABOO' (1791-1864)

HOAXER

PLAQUE: PRINCESS STREET, BEDMINSTER, BS3 4AG

One of the strangest episodes in Bristol's history is recalled by a blue plaque recording that a woman who called herself 'Princess Caraboo' lived in a terraced house in Bedminster.

The woman caused something of a sensation when she was seen wandering through the village of Almondsbury, a dozen miles or so north of Bristol, on Good Friday 1817. She was wearing a black gown, with a red and black shawl draped around her shoulders and another black shawl covering her head.

Surprised villagers watched as she knocked at the door of a cottage and spoke in a strange language to the man living there. By the gestures she made he worked out that the woman was seeking food and shelter. He took her to the home of Samuel Worrall, a magistrate, who offered her accommodation and tried to discover the woman's background.

Mr Worrall asked her to write down her native script, which he sent to language experts at Oxford University for analysis. They treated it as a joke and described it as 'humbug'. However, the woman managed to convey that she was Princess Caraboo and had been kidnapped by pirates from her home on the (non-existent) island of Javasu in the Indian Ocean. She claimed she had escaped from her kidnappers' boat by jumping overboard into the Bristol Channel and swimming ashore.

After maintaining her guise for three months Princess Caraboo was exposed as a runaway servant by her employer who had recognised her from a newspaper story. In real life Princess Caraboo was Mary Wilcox, alias Mary Baker, the daughter of a cobbler in Devon. She thought her disguise 'might make her more interesting'. On hearing this, Mr Worrall's wife paid for 'Princess Caraboo' to sail to America and start a new life.

She eventually returned to England and set up home in Bristol where she ran a business breeding leeches and selling them to hospital doctors. A blue plaque in Princess Street, Bedminster, says that 'Princess Caraboo' lived there from 1851 until her death thirteen years later. She lies at rest in an unmarked grave in Bedminster.

MARY CARPENTER (1807-1877)

SOCIAL REFORMER

PLAQUES:
THE RED LODGE, PARK ROW, BS1 5LJ
BRISTOL CATHEDRAL, BS1 5TJ

Mary Carpenter devoted much of her life to helping the poor, weak and unfortunate as a social reformer. She began by opening a Sunday school for children living in the slums of Bristol's Lewins Mead area where her father was minister of the Unitarian chapel.

By 1846 she had raised enough funds to set up what was known as a Ragged School where the children were mainly thieves and criminals. Five years later Lady Byron, widow of the poet, bought the Red Lodge, a late sixteenth-century house on Park Row, and presented it to Mary Carpenter. She turned the building into Britain's first reformatory school for the rescue and training of poor girls, some of whom were only 12 years old. Her aim was to stop them re-offending. Mary Carpenter spent twenty years working at the Red Lodge, which is now run as a museum by Bristol City Council.

She also became interested in India after meeting the reformer Raja Ram Roy when he was on a visit to Bristol where, unfortunately, he was taken ill and died. Raja Ram Roy seems to have made such an impression on Mary that she made four visits to India in the last decade of her life. Her aim was to improve the rights and conditions of children and women living there. She also campaigned for the introduction of girls' schools.

Mary Carpenter's life is commemorated in Bristol by two plaques. A blue one above the main entrance of the Red Lodge pays tribute to the work that she did there with young girls. The other plaque is in Bristol Cathedral and bears an inscription, which says that Mary Carpenter was 'foremost among the founders of reformatory and industrial schools in this city and the realm'. It also praises her for 'taking to heart the grievous lot of oriental women' and says that she awakened an 'active interest in their education and training for serious duties.'

THOMAS CHATTERTON (1752-1770)

POET

PLAQUES:
PHIPPEN STREET. BS1 6ND
ST MARY REDCLIFFE CHURCH. BS1 6RA

IN THIS HOUSE
THOMAS
CHATTERTON
1752 - 1770
POET WAS BORN

CITY AND COUNTY OF BRISTOL

Thomas Chatterton, better known as the 'boy poet', seems to be more famous for dying young after taking arsenic than for the verses he wrote. He cut short his life three months before his eighteenth birthday in apparent despair that his poetic genius had gone unrecognised in his home city of Bristol. He was buried in a paupers graveyard in central London.

Chatterton was born in a house opposite St Mary Redcliffe church, where he spent many hours studying old documents he found in the Muniment Room. From these ancient papers he taught himself to write verse in medieval English. His fertile imagination led him to create the fictional monk Thomas Rowley, whom he claimed had written the poetry two centuries earlier. Many people in the literary world were initially fooled by the so-called 'Rowley Poems' but eventually Chatterton was exposed and left Bristol for London.

Thomas Chatterton's birthplace.

After his death in a garret he became the hero of the Romantic movement and was described by the poet Samuel Taylor Coleridge as the
'wondrous boy'.

Bristol has remained largely indifferent to the 'boy poet', yet internationally
the Chatterton story triggered something of an industry devoted to remem-
bering him. A French dramatist wrote a play about Chatterton; a German
composer produced an opera about his life and American universities staged

St Mary Redcliffe church.

plays about him. Back home the poets Wordsworth and Coleridge wrote about Chatterton; artists have depicted on canvas his death in the garret, and many academic books and even a novel have been written about him.

Such was the interest in Chatterton that doctors Johnson and Boswell visited St Mary Redcliffe to see where the supposed 'Rowley manuscripts' were found.

But in Bristol, Chatterton's birthplace stood in the way of a road-widening scheme, so in the 1930s it was removed to nearby Phippen Street, where it still stands today in pointless isolation. A plaque, surmounted by Bristol's civic coat of arms, confirms that 'in this house Thomas Chatterton was born'. Next to it another plaque bears the inscription that 'this house was erected by Glen Malpas of St Thomas parish for the use of the master [Chatterton's father] of this school'.

The only remaining part of the school is one wall that has been stuck onto the side of the house and faces St Mary Redcliffe. It has its own plaque with an inscription that reads 'Thomas Chatterton attended this school'.

A statue to Chatterton was erected in 1838 in the church grounds but eight years later it was banished from consecrated land as he had taken his own life. The statue was put back some time later but was finally removed in the 1960s after being vandalised.

In the church itself a small memorial plaque on a wall in the south transept simply reads: 'Thomas Chatterton of this parish 1752–1770 poet.'

THOMAS CLARKSON (1760–1846)

ANTI-SLAVERY CAMPAIGNER

PLAQUE: THE SEVEN STARS, THOMAS LANE, REDCLIFFE, BS1 6JG

It wasn't to taste the local ale that Thomas Clarkson visited the Seven Stars public house. Instead, he was collecting evidence about the slave trade, which was then rife in Bristol. The pub's landlord, who was against slavery, took Clarkson to various dockside taverns where he met sailors who had been discharged from ships involved in the trade. Three or four slave vessels were also in port preparing for their voyages. Records show that between 1697 and 1807 more than 2,100 known ships left Bristol for the journey to collect slaves.

The testimonies that the sailors gave Clarkson enabled him to challenge the popular conception that ships involved with slavery served as a training ground for the navy. Instead he showed that seamen were often brutally treated and the ships they worked on were death traps for both enslaved Africans and the crew. Clarkson also collected iron handcuffs, branding irons and leg shackles – all items connected with the slave trade.

His meetings with sailors in the Seven Stars and other pubs had to take place under cover of darkness as much of Bristol's money was tied up with the slave trade, which, at the time, was a legal activity. Clarkson, a Cambridge-educated clergyman, passed on the information he collected to William Wilberforce MP, who led the parliamentary campaign in the latter years of the eighteenth century, which in turn led to the abolition of the Slave Trade Act of 1807.

Clarkson's visit to Bristol is marked by a multi-coloured bas-relief moulded plaque on the front of the Seven Stars, which was designed by local artist Mike Baker. It bears the heading 'Cry Freedom, Cry Seven Stars' and features a portrait of Clarkson surrounded by scenes from the anti-slavery campaign and the role which the pub played in it.

Members of Bristol Radical History Group raised several thousand pounds for the plaque, which was unveiled by Richard Hart, a civil rights lawyer from Jamaica.

Several years earlier a traditional blue plaque was erected above the pub's door. Its inscription states that Clarkson 'stayed here in 1787 to research the condition of slaves being transported'.

ARTHUR COLLINS (1885-1914)

SCHOOLBOY CRICKETER

PLAQUE: CLIFTON COLLEGE. BS8 3EZ

Cricket thrives on bizarre and brilliant achievements, probably none more so than that of a Clifton College schoolboy.

It was in June 1889 that 13-year-old Arthur E.J. Collins strode out onto the crease at the school's cricket field, known as The Close, for a junior house match. He was captain of the Clark's XI against the Junior XI of the

Upon this ground
A.E.J. COLLINS
in a junior House Match
in June 1899 scored
628 NOT OUT
THIS INNINGS IS THE HIGHEST
RECORDED IN THE HISTORY
OF CRICKET

The plaque marking
Arthur Collins' cricketing feat.

college's North Town House. Collins won the toss, put his side into bat and opened the batting himself. Remarkably, he was at the wicket for five days during which time he scored 628 runs not out. The match came to an end when there was no one left to partner Collins.

As news of his feat spread people arrived at The Close not just from other parts of Bristol but much further afield. A correspondent from *The Times* also turned up. One of his reports in the paper about the school match was headlined 'Collins Still In'. The boy's score also put him into the pages of *Wisden*, the cricketers' bible, and the *Guinness Book of Records*. It was a score that was not equalled or surpassed by any cricketer in the world until January 2016. On 4 January ABP News in India reported that 15-year-old Pranav Dhanawade amassed 652 runs in a single day. He was taking part in Mumbai's inter-school competition for the K.C. Ghandi School in Kalyan.

When Collins left Clifton College he went into the army at Woolwich Barracks, where his flair at cricket continued. He scored a century in a military match against Sandhurst.

He was commissioned into the Royal Engineers and after a posting in India was sent to France with the British Expeditionary Force. Unfortunately, he was killed on the Western Front in the first year of the First World War.

Today's cricketers at Clifton College are reminded of Collins' feat every time they step out on to The Close by a plaque there which gives details of his score and the time he spent at the crease. It proudly claims that 'this innings is the highest recorded in the history of cricket'.

RUSS CONWAY (1925-2000)

COMPOSER AND PIANIST

PLAQUE: 2 DEAN LANE, SOUTHVILLE, BS3 1DF

Nobody was more surprised than Russ Conway when his jaunty instrumental piano composition 'Side Saddle' hit the number one spot of the UK singles record charts and stayed in the top twenty for more than seven months in 1959. Shortly afterwards he followed this up with another number he called 'Roulette', which also went to the top of the charts. During a forty-year career in showbusiness Russ Conway had twenty instrumentals in the charts and sold a remarkable 30 million copies of his records. To mark his success the music industry awarded him with five gold, two platinum and two silver discs.

Russ Conway's success was notable because he never had any formal music training. He took an interest in the piano as a child while watching his mother play and was largely self-taught.

Russ Conway – his real name was Trevor Herbert Stanford – was born in Coronation Road, Southville, but when he was 4 years old his family moved to a house around the corner in Dean Lane.

After serving with both the Royal Navy and the Merchant Navy he started a musical career by playing the piano in nightclubs in London. He was soon accompanying leading singers of the day like Joan Regan, Dorothy Squires and Lita Rosa.

Russ was soon getting bookings to appear as a guest artist on various television programmes before he was offered his own series. He was also in demand for summer seasons at seaside theatres and topped the bill at pop concerts in almost every big town and city. Highlights of his career were Royal Command Performances at the London Palladium and playing for the royal family at Windsor Castle.

Russ Conway died aged 75 having suffered from cancer. At his funeral in St Mary Redcliffe church, Bristol, the pews were packed not only with family and fans but many showbusiness celebrities. The service ended with a recording of 'Side Saddle' being played.

A blue plaque which reads 'Russ Conway lived here from 1929 to 1944' is mounted on the front wall of his home in Southville.

NORAH COOKE-HURLE (1871-1960)

EDUCATIONALIST AND MENTAL HEALTH PIONEER

PLAQUE: 39 BRISLINGTON HILL, BS4 5BE

Norah Cooke-Hurle was an ardent campaigner for better services for people with learning difficulties. One of her concerns was the lack of proper schools for disabled children and the shortage of housing for those with learning difficulties.

She was a founder member of Bristol University's Council in 1909 and served on it for more than fifty years. As Norah Fry (her maiden name) she brought the cause of disabled people to the notice of the university's academics.

Norah gave a substantial amount of money to the university so that it could set up its Department of Mental Health. When the university established a centre for learning difficulties in 1988 it was named after Norah Fry. In 1918 she became the first woman councillor in Somerset and pursued her campaigning through the local authority.

Norah Fry was born in Clifton, Bristol, a member of the Quaker family that made chocolate and cocoa. She was educated at Cambridge and was one of the university's first female scholars to graduate with the equivalent of a double first.

She married Joseph Cooke-Hurle in 1915 and the couple set up home in Brislington Hill House, a prominent building in south-east Bristol which was destroyed by enemy action in the Second World War. A blue plaque honouring Norah Cooke-Hurle has been installed on the side of a retail development that now occupies the site. On it she is described as an 'Educationalist and Mental Health Pioneer'. It states that she lived at Brislington Hill House from 1915 to 1921.

JOSEPH COTTLE (1770-1853)

BOOKSELLER AND PUBLISHER

PLAQUE: HIGH STREET CORNER. BS1 2AZ

The poets William Wordsworth and Samuel Taylor Coleridge have a Bristol bookseller to thank for their big literary breakthrough. By publishing their *Lyrical Ballads* in 1798 Joseph Cottle helped to give birth to the Romantic movement in British poetry. *Lyrical Ballads* included Coleridge's *The Rime of The Ancient Mariner* and Wordsworth's *Lines Composed a Few Miles above Tintern Abbey.* He also published poems by Bristol-born Robert Southey, who became Poet Laureate, and Charles Lamb.

Yet today Joseph Cottle is virtually forgotten. There is a red plaque, of unknown origin, which honours him in the centre of Bristol. It is arguably one of the most interesting in the literary world, and marks the spot on the corner of Corn Street and High Street, in what is now fashionably called Bristol's Old Quarter, where Cottle had his bookshop at the end of the eighteenth century. The plaque tells us that besides being a bookseller Joseph Cottle was also a 'critic, publisher and poet'. It claims that he was the 'first effective publisher' of the poems of Coleridge, Southey, Lamb and Wordsworth, 'some of whose works were written here'.

Cottle ran the shop from 1791 to 1798 but continued publishing after that, offering Coleridge 1½ guineas for every 100 lines of poetry he wrote.

When Coleridge married Sarah Fricker at St Mary Redcliffe church in October 1795 Cottle set them up in their honeymoon cottage at Clevedon, Somerset, with a variety of requested household items ranging from a tin dustpan to a small tin teapot. A month later when Robert Southey married Sarah's sister, Edith, in the same church Cottle paid for the wedding ring and the marriage fees. The sisters were daughters of a sugar mould-maker of Westbury-on-Trym.

HENRY CRUGER (1739-1827)

POLITICIAN

PLAQUE: GREAT GEORGE STREET. BS1 5RR

Henry Cruger was an American who had the distinction of being both a British Member of Parliament and a member of the New York Senate. He also held a number of important roles in Bristol, including that of mayor of the city.

Cruger, who was born in New York, arrived in Bristol when he was 18 years old and set himself up as a merchant, trading as Henry Cruger and Co. He settled in the city for just over three decades.

Much of his time was devoted to civic duties. He was elected to the Bristol Common Council in 1765, a post he held for twenty-five years, and was appointed mayor in 1781. During his mayoral year of office he also held the prestigious post of Master of the Society of Merchant Venturers.

He was elected as a Member of Parliament for Bristol as a radical Whig for the first time in 1774 along with Edmund Burke. Both men were successful in the contest against two other candidates, Matthew Brickdale and Lord Clare. To mark their victory, supporters cheered them, church bells were rung and cannons fired. Cruger served a six-year parliamentary session until 1780. He was re-elected for a second session from 1784–90.

After one speech in the House of Commons on American affairs made in 1775, Cruger arrived back in Bristol in triumph. About 1,000 citizens on horseback accompanied by fifty private carriages met him at Keynsham and escorted him the 6 miles to his home in the centre of the city. Cruger was noted for speaking in Parliament about the slave trade, with which Bristol was heavily involved, urging that it would be regulated and finally abolished.

While he was living in Bristol Cruger married the daughter of Samuel Peach, a linen draper of Wine Street. He returned to New York in 1790, becoming a senator whilst remaining an alderman of the council in Bristol.

His time in Bristol is marked by a plaque, the origin of which is unknown, on the side of the house in which he lived on the corner of Great George Street and Park Street. It is engraved with the dates of the various appointments he held. The building is now a jeweller's shop.

EDWARD ST JOHN DANIEL VC (1837-1868)

ARMED FORCES OFFICER

PLAQUE: 1 WINDSOR TERRACE. CLIFTON. BS8 4LW

Edward St John Daniel was not only one of the first people to be awarded the Victoria Cross but also the youngest. He was also the first of eight men to be stripped of this prestigious honour. This followed his conviction for desertion and evading court martial.

Just before his fourteenth birthday Daniel joined HMS *Victory* as a naval cadet. Three years later he was transferred to HMS *Diamond*. He became the captain's aide-de-camp when the ship was ordered to the Black Sea at the start of the Crimean War.

Daniel was just 17 years old when he was honoured with the newly instituted Victoria Cross, the highest award for gallantry in the face of the enemy given to British and Commonwealth forces. It was awarded to him in recognition of three separate acts: he had braved heavy fire, charged enemy lines and saved the life of his commander.

Just a month after Queen Victoria had presented him with the award Daniel was reprimanded for twice being absent without leave. He was posted to South Africa where he disgraced himself by being drunk on watch. A posting to the Mediterranean followed where Daniel committed more offences and absconded before he could face his court martial. The navy declared him a deserter and expelled him from the service.

The queen later signed a royal warrant that made Daniel the first person to be stripped of the Victoria Cross.

A green plaque marking Daniel's birthplace has been installed on a house in Windsor Terrace, Clifton, by the Clifton and Hotwells Improvement Society. Apart from telling us that he was awarded the Victoria Cross the inscription doesn't give any details of his bravery or of his disgrace.

ABRAHAM DARBY (1678-1717)

IRONMASTER

PLAQUES:
ENGINEERS' WALK, ANCHOR ROAD, BS1 5LL
MILLPOND PRIMARY SCHOOL, BS5 0YR

Abraham Darby went into partnership with three other Quakers in 1702 to set up the Bristol Brass Works Company at Baptist Mills, funded by money from the slave trade. The firm became the first commercially successful brass works in Britain. With Darby at the helm it developed industrial techniques that were to revolutionise manufacturing in Britain and played a key part in the Industrial Revolution.

Darby made advances in the design of furnaces and is regarded as the first person to successfully use coke, rather than charcoal, in the smelting of iron. His brass works company saw the creation of the world's first metallurgy laboratory.

Some of the improved techniques came from a visit that Darby made to Holland, returning to Baptist Mills with Dutch workers. Along with their English counterparts they made hollowware brass pots and pans which were not only sold in England but also exported to British colonies.

Darby's brass works, powered by water from the nearby River Frome, became one of the largest industrial sites in the Bristol area.

In 1707 Darby patented an invention for 'casting bellied pots' in 'green sand' moulds, previously only used for smaller castings.

At the age of 30 Darby severed links with Baptist Mills, having taken out a lease on Coalbrookdale Works in Shropshire where iron had been smelted with charcoal since 1638. The world's first cast-iron bridge of 100ft span was designed and built in Darby's foundry at Coalbrookdale. It is still in use today as a footbridge.

Darby, who died at the age of 39, has been remembered by the Retired Professional Engineers' Club, which has installed a plaque in his honour on their wall of engineering fame in Anchor Road. There is also a plaque which is part of the Living Easton Time Signs Trail at Millpond Primary School, Baptist Mills. It depicts a scene at the brass works and was designed by local artist Mike Baker, who has given the plaque a 3D effect.

Sadly, any remains of the Baptist Mills Brass Works were destroyed with the building of Junction 3 of the M32 motorway in the 1960s.

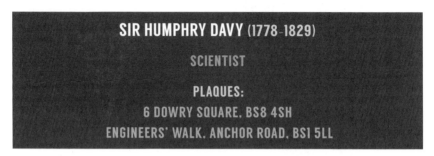

SIR HUMPHRY DAVY (1778-1829)

SCIENTIST

PLAQUES:
6 DOWRY SQUARE. BS8 4SH
ENGINEERS' WALK. ANCHOR ROAD. BS1 5LL

Humphry Davy began his scientific career when he arrived in Bristol from Penzance at the age of 19 to work for Dr Thomas Beddoes at his Pneumatic Institute. He was appointed superintendent of the institute, which was based in a house in Dowry Square, Hotwells.

The plaque commemorating Sir Humphry Davy outside the laboratory.

The laboratory where Sir Humphry Davy worked.

Davy discovered the anaesthetic effect of laughing gas (nitrous oxide), which he tested on himself and some of his friends including the poets Robert Southey and Samuel Taylor Coleridge and Peter Roget of Thesaurus fame at so-called laughing gas parties. Heating crystals of ammonium nitrate, the gas produced was collected in an oil-silk bag and inhaled through a mouthpiece. But it was some time before nitrous oxide was used in dentistry as an anaesthetic.

A paper that Davy wrote in 1799 entitled *Researches, Chemical and Physical*, led to his appointment two years later as assistant lecturer at the Royal Institute. He later became the institute's first professor of chemistry and was later appointed its president.

Davy is probably best remembered for his invention of the miners' safety lamp, which is named after him. The lamp meant that deeper, more gaseous seams could be mined with less risk of explosion, leading to greater production. Humphry Davy was knighted by the Prince Regent in 1812 for his services to science.

He suffered a stroke while in Rome and died on his way back to England at the age of 51.

Davy is commemorated by a large bronze plaque outside the Beddoes institute in Hotwells. A blue plaque, dedicated to Davy, has been erected on the engineering wall of fame in Anchor Road.

PAUL DIRAC (1902-1984)

PHYSICIST

PLAQUES:
15 MONK ROAD, BS7 8LE
ENGINEERS' WALK, ANCHOR ROAD, BS1 5LL

Little could the teachers at Bishop Road Primary School have envisaged that the boy with the aptitude for mathematics would eventually be collecting several exclusive honours in recognition of his skills. Paul Dirac's flair for maths continued at secondary school and at Bristol University, where he gained a bachelor of science degree with first class honours for both mathematics and electrical engineering. Dirac then won a scholarship to Cambridge University where he specialised in quantum mechanics – the theories which describe the behaviour of particles smaller than atoms, such as electrons.

In 1932 he was appointed as the prestigious Lucasian professor of mathematics at Cambridge, which he held for nearly forty years. One of the early holders of the post was Sir Isaac Newton.

One of the world's top honours came Dirac's way the following year when he was awarded the Nobel Prize in Physics jointly with the Austrian physicist Erwin Schrödinger, for his work in quantum mechanics.

Dirac retired from Cambridge in 1969 and moved to America where he lectured at Florida State University. During the next twelve years he wrote more than sixty papers. In 1973 Paul Dirac became a member of one of the most exclusive groups in England when the queen admitted him to the Order of Merit. This special honour is awarded to people of great achievement in the fields of arts, learning, literature and science. It is the sole gift of the sovereign and goes to a small and select band of people.

Paul Dirac died in Tallahassee in 1984 at the age of 82. After his death a blue plaque was unveiled outside Dirac's birthplace in Bishopston, by the Lord Mayor of Bristol. The Retired Professional Engineers' Club has also honoured him with a plaque on its engineering wall of fame in Anchor Road.

ELIZA WALKER DUNBAR (1845-1925)

PHYSICIAN

PLAQUE: 9 OAKFIELD ROAD, BS8 2AJ

More than a century before women were talking about breaking through the so-called glass ceiling to get to the top of their professions, Dr Eliza Walker Dunbar was well on her way there. At the time medicine in England was very much a male-only profession. Much courage was needed by women like Miss Dunbar to break through the rigid conventions of the time.

To achieve her ambition of becoming a doctor Dunbar, who came from a medical family, studied at Zurich University where she graduated in medicine in 1872. The following year she was appointed Bristol's first female resident house surgeon at the city's Hospital for Sick Children.

When an Enabling Act was passed in Parliament in 1876 the King and Queen's College of Physicians, Ireland, admitted women to its examinations. Dr Dunbar, alongside four other women, obtained the qualification of the college which entitled her to register her degree and diplomas in the Medical Register of the UK.

With other supporters of women's' independence, Eliza Walker Dunbar helped her friend Lucy Read establish the Read Dispensary for Women and Children at Hotwells, in 1874. As well as working in private practice, Dr Eliza Walker Dunbar and some friends later started the Bristol Private Hospital for Women and Children in Berkeley Square, Clifton. Bristol was then the only city outside London to have a hospital offering treatment for women given by women.

Eliza Walker Dunbar died after a fall at her home when she was 80, having spent more than fifty years in the medical profession. At the time of her death she was still on the staff of the hospital that she co-founded.

Her life and work is commemorated by a Clifton and Hotwells Improvement Society green plaque that has been installed at her home in Oakfield Road, Clifton, where she also carried on her private practice. It was unveiled by the late Dr Beryl Corner, another leading female pioneer in the medical field in Bristol.

SIR ROY FEDDEN (1885-1973)

AIRCRAFT ENGINEER

PLAQUE: ENGINEERS' WALK. ANCHOR ROAD. BS1 5LL

After completing his engineering apprenticeship Bristol-born Roy Fedden designed a complete car. He may have been inspired by the fact that his father owned a French Deauville motorcar which was one of the first motor vehicles to be registered in the Bristol area. Whatever thoughts Fedden might have had about a career in motor engineering they were changed by the First World War.

Instead, he went into aircraft engineering and for twenty-two years was chief engineer with the Bristol Aeroplane Company. During this time, the company produced a range of now-famous aircraft engines including the Mercury, Pegasus, Perseus, Taurus, Hercules and Centaurus. Fedden's fame spread worldwide as he made advances in aircraft engines.

During the Second World War he was special advisor to the minister of Aircraft Production for three years and recommended the creation of a postgraduate college of aeronautics, which came into being at Cranfield University in 1946. Fedden was involved with the college, either as a teacher or governor, until 1969.

Roy Fedden was three times president of the Aeronautical Society – in 1938, 1939 and 1945 – and was knighted in 1942. A blue plaque honouring him can be found on the Retired Professional Engineers' Club wall of fame on Anchor Road.

KEITH FLOYD (1943–2009)

RESTAURATEUR AND INNKEEPER

PLAQUE:
112 PRINCESS VICTORIA STREET,
BS8 4DB

Clifton and Hotwells
THE SITE OF KEITH FLOYD'S FIRST BISTRO 1969-1972
Improvement Society

Keith Floyd would have been one of the last people to ever dream of his name appearing on a commemorative plaque. But one was unveiled on the exterior of his first restaurant a year after his death. It simply records that Floyd's Bistro traded at Princess Victoria Street from 1969–72. He later opened other restaurants in Clifton and Redland.

Floyd soon became known for the eccentric manner in which he ran his restaurants. He thought nothing, for example, of leaving his bistro while a meal was cooking to pop into the local pub for a glass of wine and exchange banter with the 'regulars' and then return to his kitchen.

He became a flamboyant television chef after being 'spotted' by a BBC producer who dined at one of his restaurants. Floyd was always seen on television wearing a bow tie and enjoying a tipple or two of wine whilst preparing and cooking a dish. He worked without a script and barked orders to the cameraman who was filming him. All this seemed to endear him to a nationwide audience. From the 1980s onwards he made twenty-six series of television programmes, some of six episodes and others of twelve. He filmed one series in India.

Floyd also owned gastro pubs and wrote cookery books and several autobiographies but financially he eventually lost everything. Explaining his financial downfall he once admitted that whilst he enjoyed cooking he was no businessman.

Despite the fortune that he had made Keith Floyd left just £7,500 in his will. His son and daughter were reported as being sole beneficiaries to his estate. His fourth and last wife, Tess, told a national newspaper that his 'heavy drinking, his eating and chaotic finances' all took their toll.

Keith Floyd died of a heart attack at the Dorset home of his partner Celia Martin on 14 September 2009 after a meal of oysters and partridge with champagne. A year later, former restaurant staff, customers and fans gathered in Clifton on a wet morning for the unveiling of his memorial plaque, which had been installed by the Clifton and Hotwells Improvement Society.

WILLIAM FRIESE-GREENE (1855-1921)

CINEMATOGRAPHY PIONEER

PLAQUES:
CITY HALL, BS1 5TR
QUEENS ROAD, BS8 1QU

Bristolians like to think that it was a son of their city who invented moving pictures, but Americans prefer to differ. However, there are two plaques in Bristol which honour William Friese-Greene as a 'pioneer of cinematography'. One of them was unveiled amidst much civic pomp and ceremony by the Lord Mayor.

Friese-Greene was born at College Street, close to Bristol Cathedral, and was educated at the nearby Queen Elizabeth's Hospital. He began work with a photographer in Clifton. A plaque outside an office in the Queens Road shopping centre at Clifton states that the 'inventor of moving pictures' served a 'six-year apprenticeship here' from 1869. Friese-Greene went on to open his own photographic studio next to the Victoria Rooms nearby and later moved to Bath where he opened a studio, which he called the Photographic Institute. A studio in London followed.

Throughout his career Friese-Greene took out seventy-eight British patents for his inventions. Amongst other things he had been developing a process for producing photographic cigarette cards and was developing an X-ray examination system. In the 1880s he designed a camera that would expose a series of photographs for projection by lantern slides, creating the illusion of moving film. He invented what he called a 'new photographic today'. This was described as a series of pictures on a strip of film which, when turned by a handle, would move. Friese-Greene thought this invention might be useful to the War Office in the photography of battles. However, he spent many thousands of pounds trying to interest others in his projects, which led to him being declared bankrupt in 1891.

He died at the age of 66 whilst he was speaking at a conference about film in London. It is said that he had just 1s 10d in his pockets – which happened to be the price of a cinema ticket at the time. When his funeral took place cinemas all over Britain stopped screening their films and held a two-minute silence, allowing filmgoers to pay their respects to Friese-Greene.

In 1955, on what would have been Friese-Greene's hundredth birthday, the Lord Mayor of Bristol, surrounded by other civic dignitaries, unveiled a plaque on Friese-Greene's birthplace. The inscription on it described Friese-Greene as 'the pioneer of cinematography'. But the plaque didn't stay in position for long for the city council demolished the houses in College Street to make way for a redevelopment scheme. The plaque can now be seen on the rear wall of City Hall, the headquarters of the city council, facing what was the photographer's birthplace.

JOHN FROST (1784–1877)

POLITICAL LEADER

PLAQUE: 68 PARK ROAD. BS16 1AU

Tailor and draper John Frost, the Mayor of Newport, Monmouth, in 1836 became a leader of the Chartists, an early working-class socialist movement that started at the beginning of Queen Victoria's reign.

Frost led campaigns for the rights of working people and after leading a Chartist uprising in Newport he was sentenced to be hanged, drawn and quartered. The sentence was commuted to transportation for life to Tasmania, where Frost was eventually given an unconditional pardon. He returned to England in 1855 and lived out his old age in a cottage in Park Road, Stapleton. A plaque on the building describes him as a Chartist leader and social revolutionary who lived in the cottage for twenty-two years.

In his will Frost left instructions that he should be buried beside his wife and son in the graveyard at nearby Horfield parish church. The weather-beaten headstone on his grave was replaced in the 1980s with a new one which was unveiled by the Labour politician Neil Kinnock, who regarded Frost as a hero. The replacement headstone had been made with the help of a grant from Newport City Council.

EDWARD WILLIAM GODWIN (1833-1886)

ARCHITECT

PLAQUE: 21 PORTLAND SQUARE. BS2 8SJ

William Godwin was an architect, theatre critic and man of many other artistic parts who caused a scandal among polite society by running away with married actress Ellen Terry.

Godwin, who was born in Bristol, started work when he was 15 years old in a surveyor's office in St Pauls. Six years later he set up his own architectural practice and became known for his use of round-headed arches, arcades and decorative brickwork. The ground-floor arches of the carriage works at Stokes Croft, now on English Heritage's list of buildings at risk, were originally for access by the carriages built there. Godwin's village hall at Westbury-on-Trym is still standing, as are a couple of his semi-detached villas in Sneyd Park. He was also involved with the nineteenth-century restoration of St Mary Redcliffe church.

When he set up home in Portland Square, St Pauls, Godwin cleared the house of Victorian furniture and filled it with Japanese-style decor. His home was believed to be the only such decorated house in the country.

Godwin also designed furniture and fabric as well as costumes for actors. He was also a theatre critic for the *Western Daily Press*. It was while he was working in the theatre that Godwin met the actress Ellen Terry, who was married to the artist G.F. Watts. However, Miss Terry and Godwin had a six-year affair during which time she had two children by him. He designed her costumes when she was appearing at the Theatre Royal in King Street.

During the relatively short time Godwin lived in Portland Square the house had become something of a social centre for the artistic and literary set. He later moved to London where he set up an architectural practice and was commissioned by the painter James Whistler to build his White House in Chelsea.

A blue plaque commemorating Godwin's life can be found on the house in which he lived at Portland Square with Ellen Terry from 1862–65.

CATHERINE GRACE OBE (1907-1986)

EDUCATIONAL PIONEER

PLAQUE: UPPER BELGRAVE ROAD, BS8 2XL

Catherine Grace would have probably found it difficult to envisage that the special school she founded in a rented room at the end of the Second World War would one day be expanded to occupy several buildings set in 6 acres of grounds on the edge of Clifton and Durdham Downs.

Miss Grace, as she was known, never had any children of her own although she had experience as both a teacher and a medical secretary at a hospital for people with special needs. She opened St Christopher's School in 1945, because she felt she had to do something for children with learning difficulties and those with physical disabilities or emotional problems. Miss Grace's aim was to educate and care for those described in her day as 'non-educable'.

She opened her school with just six children and ran it on the principles of Dr Rudolph Steiner, a philosopher who believed that children's creative, spiritual and moral dimensions need as much attention as their intellectual ones. Miss Grace believed that his ideas were the key to liberating the personality. At one point when the school had 170 pupils it was the largest in Britain for children with learning difficulties.

At the end of 2015 the school's trustees announced that pupil numbers had dwindled to thirty-eight and, because of financial problems, the school would have to close at Easter 2016. However, a new group providing special education and care services has since taken over St Christopher's.

In recognition of her work Catherine Grace was awarded an OBE in 1972. She has also been honoured with a blue plaque on the front of her home overlooking Clifton Downs. The inscription describes Miss Grace as an 'educational pioneer' and says that 'she lived in this house'.

WILLIAM GILBERT GRACE (1848-1915)

DOCTOR AND SPORTSMAN

PLAQUES:
EASTON LEISURE CENTRE. BS5 0SW
15 VICTORIA SQUARE. BS8 4ES

Although he qualified and practised as a doctor William Gilbert Grace, or W.G. as he was universally known, is best remembered for his cricketing skills rather than his use of his stethoscope. He was born into a cricketing family and played his first game for West Gloucestershire against Bedminster when he was 9 years old. Just six years later he turned out for Bristol XI against the England XI on the Downs. Along with his brothers he played for Gloucestershire County Cricket Club, making it one of the strongest teams in the country in the late 1800s. W.G. was the team's captain from the club's inception in 1870 until the end of the century.

He is famous for once supposedly refusing to leave the crease after being given out leg before wicket, telling the umpire: 'They came to see me bat, not you umpire.'

He was the first man to score 100 first-class hundreds. In total he made 126 first-class centuries, scored 54,896 first class runs and took nearly 3,000 wickets.

It took Grace eleven years to qualify as a doctor because his cricketing interests intervened and took him all over the country. So it was that he started medical training when he was aged 20 at the Bristol Medical School and qualified at St Bartholomew's Hospital, London.

In 1879 W.G. opened a surgery on Stapleton Road, Easton, which he ran for fifteen years. During the summer he often had to employ a locum to run the practice while he was playing cricket either on a pitch at home or away. He was quickly on the scene though after an explosion at Easton colliery in 1886 when eight miners lost their lives. Dr Grace was able to treat some of the injured men. When he moved to Victoria Square in Clifton Grace still kept his surgery at Easton and walked there and back every day. He retired from medicine in 1898 although it was another ten years before he played his last game of first-class cricket.

It may not be generally known that Grace was also enthusiastic about bowling and was the founder of the English Bowling Association in 1903. He was elected its first president. His interest in both cricket and bowling is featured on a bas-relief moulded commemorative plaque in the car park of Easton Leisure Centre, which stands on the site of Grace's surgery. The text describes him as 'a well-known and respected local doctor who cared greatly for the people of Easton and surrounding area'. This multi-coloured plaque, designed by local artist Mike Baker, is part of the Easton Living Times Sign Trail. Unusually for a plaque, it has wording in Braille for the visually impaired. The Clifton and Hotwells Improvement Society have erected one of their green plaques outside Grace's home in Victoria Square. It says he lived in this grand four-storey corner house from 1894–96.

FRANCIS GREENWAY (1777-1837)

ARCHITECT

THE MALL, CLIFTON, BS8 4DS
THE GALLERIES, BS1 3XD

Francis Greenway is probably the only criminal to have his portrait on a banknote and to have two plaques in his honour featured on prominent buildings in the same city.

Greenway was born into a family of builders and stonemasons at Mangotsfield near Bristol. He trained as an architect under John Nash, who was responsible for much of Regency London under the patronage of the Prince of Wales, later George IV. After his training, Greenway set up his own architectural practice and secured many commissions in Bath and Bristol. However, his only known remaining construction in the United Kingdom is the building in The Mall, Clifton, which is now the home of the Clifton Club, a private members' club founded in 1818.

It was built between 1806–09 as a hotel and assembly room. A young Princess Victoria and her mother, the Duchess of Kent, spent a night there in October 1830 during a visit to the West Country.

Greenway went bankrupt and in 1812 pleaded guilty to forging a promissory note for £250. A judge sentenced him to death but Greenway was later granted a reprieve and transported to Australia for fourteen years.

Far from being a punishment, it seems that transportation turned out to be the making of Greenway as an architect. He came to the notice of the Governor of Sydney, which led to his appointment as a government architect. Greenway went on to build some of Sydney's main public buildings including its law courts, churches and even the Parliament building. The Australian government was so impressed with Greenway's work that it later featured his portrait on a $10 note. Greenway died in Australia aged 60 never having returned to his native West Country.

In Bristol in 2008 the Clifton and Hotwells Improvement Society recognised Greenway's architectural skills by installing a commemorative plaque at the entrance to the Clifton Club. Greenway's imposing

The Clifton Club.

building on The Mall, with its ionic columns, still stands out as a remarkable landmark in a street packed with boutiques, restaurants and bars all with nondescript facades. The inscription on the plaque says that he became known as 'the Father of Australian architecture'. It was unveiled by the Australian High Commissioner and replaced an earlier one. A second plaque commemorating Greenway has been erected at one of the entrances to The Galleries shopping centre in Broadmead. It stands on the site of Newgate Prison where he languished while waiting to be transported.

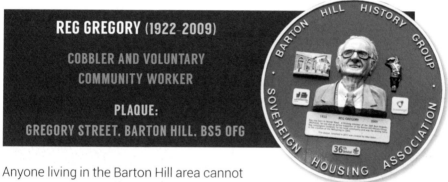

REG GREGORY (1922–2009)

COBBLER AND VOLUNTARY COMMUNITY WORKER

PLAQUE:
GREGORY STREET, BARTON HILL, BS5 0FG

Anyone living in the Barton Hill area cannot easily forget Reg Gregory. Not only did he live his entire life in the area but a street has been named in his honour and there's also a plaque helping to keep his name alive.

Reg Gregory, who was a cobbler by trade, devoted much of his time to helping those who lived and worked in Barton Hill and the nearby neighbourhoods of Redfield and St George. He helped to shape the lives of hundreds of boys through more than fifty years of service with the Boys' Brigade. He joined the unit attached to the local Methodist church when he was 12 years old and worked his way up through the ranks to become a captain, a post he held for fifteen years.

Reg Gregory spent decades as a trade unionist helping to improve the lot of his fellow workers and also served as a magistrate in Bristol for many years until he was 70, when he had to step down from the main list of justices. He then transferred to the Judiciary Supplemental List which meant sitting in court as and when his services were needed. When he was in his eighties he became chairman of the Healthy Places, Happy People project in Barton Hill.

In recognition of his life-long work with the community Reg Gregory was presented with the Lord Mayor of Bristol's Medal in 2006. He died three years later aged 87.

When parts of Barton Hill were regenerated, a cul-de-sac, which was created as part of the new Sovereign Homes development, was named after Reg Gregory in 2012. The following year a bas-relief multi-coloured plaque commemorating him was commissioned by Barton Hill History Group. Reg had been a member for more than twenty years, earning himself an honorary membership through his input and enthusiasm. Artist Mike Baker, who designed the plaque, made a portrait of Reg its centrepiece. It is surrounded by illustrations and text highlighting various aspects of his life. The plaque, sponsored by Sovereign Housing, was unveiled in, appropriately, Gregory Street.

ELSIE GRIFFIN (1895-1989)

INTERNATIONAL OPERA SINGER

PLAQUE: ST MICHAEL'S ON THE MOUNT PRIMARY SCHOOL, BS2 8BE

It could be said that Elsie Griffin's musical career began when she was a child singing on stage in Bristol and winning awards at the city's annual music festival.

However, she made her professional debut as a singer entertaining British troops in France in the First World War, having joined a concert party which had been formed at the request of King George V. Elsie popularised two songs which had been written by Bristol barrister Fred Weatherly, 'Roses of Picardy' and 'Danny Boy'.

In 1919 she joined the D'Oyly Carte Opera Company, quickly becoming known for her performances in the soprano roles of Gilbert and Sullivan operas like *The Gondoliers*, *Yeomen of the Guard* and *The Pirates of Penzance*. It was while she was singing with the D'Oyly Carte Company that she met her future husband, Ivan Menzies, who was known for his comic baritone roles.

Elsie left the D'Oyly Carte in 1926 and was soon in demand by the BBC both as a solo artist and with her husband in comic duets. Her recording of 'Poor Wandering One' from *The Pirates of Penzance* was voted the best

British gramophone solo of the year in 1929. Elsie went on to tour in South Africa in Gilbert and Sullivan operas and later travelled around the world with her husband in various concert performances. Such was her professionalism that despite chronic illness, Elsie, with her husband, took part in the D'Oyly Carte Opera Company's centennial season, in 1975, in the final performance of *Trial By Jury*.

Elsie Griffin died fourteen years later in Surrey at the age of 94. She is remembered in Bristol by a blue plaque at St Michael's on the Mount Primary School, St Michael's Hill, which was unveiled by the Lord Mayor. The plaque simply states that Elsie was a pupil at the school and 'lived nearby'. Her childhood home was on St Michael's Hill.

SARAH (1770-1852) AND THOMAS GUPPY

INVENTOR AND ENGINEER RESPECTIVELY

PLAQUES:
7 RICHMOND HILL, CLIFTON, BS8 1AT
8-10 BERKELEY SQUARE, BS8 1HH

Sarah Guppy was never short of an idea. She was taking out patents for her inventions for a large part of her life. Indeed, she registered her final patent when she was 74 years old – a method of making ships waterproof.

One of her patents concerned a method of making safe piling for bridges; this came some twenty years before Isambard Kingdom Brunel had thought of building his bridge across the River Avon at Clifton.

Another patent concerned 'Certain improvements in tea and coffee urns, whereby it is possible to cook one or more eggs in the vapour arising there from through suspending a small vessel of such form and size as may suit the said purpose'.

Sarah also designed a metal-framed four-poster bed, with drawers beneath which converted into steps for exercise. Across the top of the bed was an exercise bar.

Another of her ideas was a method of keeping ships free of barnacles, which led to her receiving a £40,000 government contract. She also came up with a design for a candlestick that made candles burn longer.

When Sarah moved from Queen Square, in the centre of the city, to Clifton she took out a lease on the land opposite her new home in Richmond Hill. This was so that it would remain a green space for the enjoyment of people living in Clifton. The land, surrounded by trees, is still largely open, despite efforts in the 1980s by Bristol City Council to turn it into a car park.

In 2006 a descendant of Sarah's unveiled a plaque commemorating her life and work, which had been installed by Clifton and Hotwells Improvement Society outside her former home. It states that Sarah Guppy 'lived here from 1841–52'.

Her son, Thomas, who was an engineer, was a close friend of Isambard Kingdom Brunel. The two men, with other investors, formed the Great Western Steamship Company. Guppy also contributed to Brunel's designs for the SS *Great Western* and the SS *Great Britain* and worked with him on building the Great Western Railway from Bristol to London.

Thomas Guppy is commemorated by a green plaque donated by Clifton and Hotwells Improvement Society. It is mounted on the house in Berkeley Square, Clifton, in which he lived from 1835–39. The building is now occupied by Bristol University.

EDDIE HAPGOOD (1908-1973)

PROFESSIONAL FOOTBALLER

PLAQUE: HAPGOOD STREET, BS5 0DD

The inscription on a plaque in Barton Hill describes Eddie Hapgood as 'Bristol's greatest footballer'. However, he never turned out for either of the city's professional football clubs. He did have a trial though with Bristol Rovers in a Western League match for the reserve team and was offered a contract of £8 a week. But Hapgood turned down the offer because he would have had to drive a coal lorry for one of the club's directors during the summer season. He preferred to work on a relative's delivery round driving a milk cart.

A Bristol Rovers' scout had spotted Hapgood when he was playing for his local side, St Philips Adult Juniors. The team was part of the Bristol Downs

League, a standalone league that is still running today but does not feed into the English Football League system.

However, within a year of his trial with Rovers Hapgood was playing for Kettering Town in the Southern League but only made twelve appearances for the club before being recruited by Arsenal in the football league. Hapgood played for the London club from 1927 to 1945, making a total of 434 appearances in league and cup games. He was in the Arsenal side that won five league titles and the FA Cup twice. Besides captaining Arsenal, Hapgood also had the distinction of being captain for England, both in the 1930s.

After retiring as a player Hapgood moved into football management with several clubs including Blackburn Rovers, Waterford and Bath City before permanently hanging up his boots.

Eddie Hapgood – his real name was Edris – was the ninth of ten children, six girls and four boys. He was born in the area of St Philips known as The Dings. When he was 6 years old his family moved to nearby Ranelagh Street, Barton Hill. Hapgood is still regarded by local people as a sporting hero and a bas-relief moulded plaque commemorating his sporting career was unveiled by his son Michael in 2003 on what would have been Eddie Hapgood's 95th birthday. The plaque is unusual in that it has a 3D image of Hapgood in action on the football pitch. On each side of him are the team badges of England and Arsenal. The plaque was erected in Hapgood Street, which was named after the footballer as part of a regeneration scheme in Barton Hill. The plaque was installed by the Barton Hill History Group and designed by local artist Mike Baker.

RUBY HELDER (1890–1938)

INTERNATIONAL OPERA STAR

PLAQUE: FLATS AT SOUTHERN END OF EASTON ROAD. BS5 0EX

Ruby Helder was affectionately known as the Lady Tenor. She was the world's only female professional tenor singer with an extraordinary two octave vocal range from C to high C. Enrico Caruso, the renowned Italian opera singer, reckoned her range of two octaves was only two notes short of his own. He introduced Ruby to the Metropolitan Opera House, New York, where the American audiences took the British singer to their hearts.

She was born Emma Jane Holder but adopted her stage name when she found that someone else in her singing class had the same surname.

As a child she used to entertain customers in her father's Glasshouse public house at Lawrence Hill. She was encouraged to take formal singing lessons and trained at the Guildhall School of Music, London. Ruby made her first public appearance on the operatic stage at the Queen's Hall, London, when she was 19 years old. It wasn't long before she was offered recording contracts and invited to sing at concert halls around the world.

Ruby toured America and Canada with John Philip Sousa and his band, which was known for military marches. She made popular the song 'Come into the Garden Maud', the words of which were based on a song from *Maude* by Alfred Tennyson.

In America she met her husband-to-be, the artist and architect Chesley Bonestell. After their marriage the couple toured Italy before returning to live in America. As Ruby's popularity was on the wane she took up teaching music and retired from singing in 1935. She died three years later, aged 48, in a Hollywood hotel after fighting a long battle against alcoholism.

A plaque commemorating her life and career was unveiled by the Lord Mayor of Bristol in 2001. As her birthplace had been demolished in the middle of the 1960s for a major road scheme the plaque was fixed to a block of flats in nearby Walker Close at the southern end of Easton Road. Unfortunately, a tree now obscures this memorial to a popular star.

GERTRUDE HERMES (1901–1983)

ARTIST AND SCULPTOR

PLAQUE: 5 SION HILL, BS8 4BA

The name of Gertrude Hermes is not generally known today although she had an international reputation as an artist, wood-engraver and sculptor. Her work went on show at major exhibitions in many countries and she produced a commission for the British Pavilion at the Paris World Fair in 1937. Two years later she was selected to represent Great Britain at the prestigious Venice Biennial Exhibition. The work of Gertrude Hermes is also included in collections at the Victoria and Albert Museum, the British Museum, the National Portrait and Tate Galleries in London.

Gertrude also had the distinction of having her engravings used in the first issues of the Penguin Classics books. Such was her talent that she was elected a full member of the Royal Academy in 1971. She was awarded an OBE in 1981.

Gertrude Hermes trained in London alongside the sculptor Henry Moore and the artist Blair Hughes-Stanton, whom she married in 1926. However, the couple divorced seven years later.

When the Clifton and Hotwells Improvement Society erected a green plaque on her home in Sion Hill, Clifton, one of the speakers at the unveiling ceremony described Gertrude as 'one of Bristol's most treasured artists and deserved the recognition of a plaque'. Its inscription says that she died at her home aged 82.

RICHARD HILL (1838-1869)

POLICE CONSTABLE

PLAQUE: TRINITY ROAD POLICE STATION. BS2 0NW

Policeman Richard Hill was stabbed to death while trying to intervene in an argument between several men, one of them drunk, over the ill-treatment of a donkey. The incident happened in Gloucester Lane off Old Market Street and carried over into a pub where PC Hill was stabbed in the thigh by one of the men who was armed with a knife. He died from loss of blood.

The murder shocked the people of Bristol. Tens of thousands of mourners lined the streets as PC Hill's cortege made its way from Trinity church, Old Market, to the cemetery at Arnos Vale where he was buried with full honours. Immediately behind the hearse walked six young policemen who shared lodgings with Richard Hill. They were followed by Hill's bride-to-be, who was to have married the murdered 31-year-old policeman later that week. She was followed by uniformed constables, sergeants and inspectors.

A marble memorial plaque to Richard Hill is in the main reception area of Trinity Road police station, close to the scene of the murder. The text says that PC Hill was 'murdered in the execution of his duty on 24 April 1869'. It goes on to say that the plaque 'was erected as a mark of esteem by his brother officers and inhabitants of the city'.

SIR STANLEY HOOKER (1907-1984)

AIRCRAFT ENGINE DESIGNER

PLAQUE: ENGINEERS' WALK. ANCHOR ROAD. BS1 5LL

Sir Stanley Hooker was one of Britain's greatest aero-engine designers who designed the engines for the world's first supersonic aircraft, the Concorde.

Another of his main achievements was the performance development of the Rolls-Royce Merlin engine, which was used in the Hurricane and Spitfire fighters during the Battle of Britain in the Second World War. The Spitfire was the most famous of Britain's aircraft in the war. He also designed the engines for the Harrier jump jet, which was used in the Falklands War in 1982.

Sir Stanley joined Rolls-Royce in 1938 and took charge of the company's early work on jet engines, which were developed from the original design of Sir Frank Whittle. He was appointed technical director of the Bristol Engine Division of Rolls-Royce in 1966 and retired four years later. However, he was called back to work in the following year to rescue the troubled RB-211 engine project. He was knighted in 1974 for his services to the aircraft industry.

Sir Stanley died aged 76 in hospital in Bristol after a long illness. His death came on the day his autobiography *Not Much of An Engineer* was published. In memory of him the Retired Professional Engineers' Club erected a blue plaque on their engineers' wall of fame on Anchor Road. It was sponsored by Rolls-Royce and lists some of the aero-engine projects with which he was involved.

BOB HOPE (1903-2003)

COMEDIAN AND ACTOR

PLAQUE: ST GEORGE PARK, (CHURCH ROAD ENTRANCE), BS5 7AA

It's little known that Bob Hope — yes, that Bob Hope, the popular entertainer — spent part of his childhood in Bristol. His family moved from London to Bristol in 1906 and lived for about two years in the Whitehall and St George districts of the city before emigrating to Ohio in America. Bob Hope became an American citizen in 1920.

Bob Hope's career in the world of showbusiness began in vaudeville and then he became a dancer and comedian on the American stage. He made his Broadway debut in *The Sidewalks of New York* in 1927. Hope became a popular radio and television performer and also appeared in many films, six of them with Bing Crosby and Dorothy Lamour.

During the Second World War and the conflicts in Korea and Vietnam, Bob Hope spent much time raising the morale of the troops with his comedy act.

Hope didn't forget Bristol, although he would have only been about 3 years old when he lived there. On a visit to the city in 1952 he asked his chauffeur to take him to St George so that he could see his old home.

In 2004, a year after Bob Hope died at the age of 100, a bas-relief moulded plaque depicting the entertainer was unveiled on a pillar at the main entrance to St George Park where he had played as a child. It was designed by local artist Mike Baker and created by the Living Easton team. It was unveiled by British comedian Eddie Large of the showbusiness comedy duo Little and Large.

LESLIE HOWARD (1893-1943)

ACTOR

PLAQUE: BRISTOL AIRPORT, LULSGATE, BS48 3DY

A plaque on a wall at Bristol Airport says it was installed 'in memory of those who never returned'. It is a tribute to the four-man crew and thirteen passengers on board a plane that was due to land at Bristol Airport, which was then situated at Whitchurch 3 miles south of the city, on 1 June 1943. Unfortunately, it was attacked in mid-flight and shot down.

To this day mystery surrounds the incident although there are several theories. One of them is that the Germans thought that the British Prime Minister Winston Churchill was on board; another was that several of the passengers were spies.

The passengers included Leslie Howard, the film and stage actor who appeared in such films as *Gone With the Wind* and *The Scarlet Pimpernel*. Also on board was a mother with her two daughters aged 11 and 18 months. Their plane, a Douglas DC3, which was on a flight from Lisbon, was attacked by eight Junkers Ju 88 German fighter aircraft and was shot down over the Bay of Biscay.

In 1957 the airport moved from Whitchurch to Lulsgate, 7 miles south of Bristol city centre. It was there that the Lord Mayor unveiled the memorial plaque on the sixty-seventh anniversary of the crash in 2010. It had been organised by a relative of one of the victims.

VICTORIA HUGHES (1897-1978)

TOILET ATTENDANT

PLAQUE:
STOKE ROAD, CLIFTON AND DURDHAM
DOWNS. BS9 1FG

Victoria Hughes
1897 - 1978
Who befriended and cared for prostitutes when she worked here as a lavatory attendant from 1929 to 1962

To the passer-by a particular single-storey green and white painted building surrounded by trees and bushes looks like a bungalow in the countryside. But appearances can be deceiving for this is a ladies' public toilet on Clifton and Durdham Downs, 440 acres of wooded and open country in the north of the city. A blue plaque above the door honours Victoria Hughes who, for more than three decades, worked here as a toilet attendant. She is quite possibly the only 'loo attendant', as she preferred to be known, in the country to be remembered in such a way.

Her official duties included issuing tickets, cleaning the premises and selling sanitary supplies for which she was paid in cash every Thursday. When she took on the job in 1929 Victoria's pay packet was £2 2s a week.

The toilets on Clifton Down where Victoria Hughes worked.

Unexpected national fame came her way at the age of 80 when she published her memoirs, *Ladies Mile*. In this slim publication Victoria revealed that she was a confidante of the prostitutes who plied their trade along Ladies Mile, a road crossing the Downs. The name reflects not only the length of the road but the fact that at one time local society ladies rode their horses there.

In her book Mrs Hughes disclosed that she invited the prostitutes into her small office and offered them a cup of tea, sympathy and advice, especially if they had been badly treated by their clients. Victoria made notes of conversations she had with the women, who often told her why they had resorted to the 'world's oldest profession' or about any problems they had at home.

In *Ladies Mile*, which was serialised by Victoria Hughes' local paper, she wrote: 'They in turn, gave me a sort of companionship and warmth. My job was to take the pennies and not to moralise. I'll leave others to huff and puff about what went on.' She described herself as a 'homely little housewife' who attended church fellowship meetings.

A national newspaper published extracts of Victoria's book when it was published in 1977. It was reported that civic dignitaries in Bristol were shocked by the revelations of the toilet attendant. Her book had lifted the lid on a hitherto hidden aspect of social life in this middle-class area of the city. However, since then it has come to be regarded as a valuable contribution to Bristol's social history.

The blue plaque was unveiled in 2003 by the Deputy Lord Mayor of Bristol. The inscription on it says that Victoria 'befriended and cared for prostitutes'.

SIR HENRY IRVING (1838–1905)

ACTOR

PLAQUE: PICTON STREET, BS2 8EZ

John Henry Brodribb, who was born in the Somerset village of Keinton Mandeville, the son of a shopkeeper, became the greatest English actor of his time – but not by that name. For stage purposes he adopted the name of Henry Irving.

His family moved to Bristol when he was a small boy and lived at 1 Wellington Place, at the corner of Picton Street and Ashley Road.

Although he made his stage debut in 1856 it was ten years before he made his first appearance in London. In 1895 Henry Irving became the first actor to be knighted.

Irving was actor-manager at the Lyceum Theatre, London, for more than twenty years. During this time he played most of the great Shakespearean roles. Many of them were during a theatrical partnership with his leading lady on the stage, the actress Ellen Terry. During his career Irving played more than 600 roles.

A bronze plaque on a house in Picton Street, Stokes Croft, bears the inscription 'Henry Irving actor lived here'. Although there are no dates on the plaque it is believed that Irving resided there as a child. During a speech he made at a banquet in his honour in Bristol a year before his death, Irving recalled being taken at the age of 5 to see the launching of Brunel's steamship the SS *Great Britain*. This took place in Bristol harbour in 1843. Irving was reported in a newspaper as saying, 'Although I cannot claim to belong to Bristol, here I spent some of my youngest days'.

He died in Bradford aged 67 and his remains were buried in Westminster Abbey.

SAMUEL JACKSON (1794-1869)

ARTIST

PLAQUE: 8 CANYNGE SQUARE, BS8 3LA

Samuel Jackson was a watercolour artist who was part of the Bristol School, an informal group of amateur and professional artists working in the city in the early nineteenth century. He is known for painting the Bristol scene, notably romantic watercolours of the Avon Gorge, Sea Mills and Clifton.

Jackson was a friend of Isambard Kingdom Brunel and was commissioned to paint the construction of the Clifton Suspension Bridge so that the public could understand the general effect it would have on the Avon Gorge. Many of Jackson's works can be seen in the City Museum and Art Gallery.

He first put his works on show in 1823 at an exhibition held by the Society of Painters in Oil and Watercolours. The following year he was responsible for curating the first Bristol Artists' Exhibition at the new Bristol Institution. A few years later he was instrumental in the organisation of an exhibition staged by the Bristol Society of Artists.

Jackson never moved from Bristol where he was born. He lived at various addresses in the city, at Hotwells, Cotham and Canynge Square, Clifton. A plaque on a house in the square states that he lived there from 1843–69. At the time Canynge Square was known as Cambridge Place. Jackson died there aged 75 and was buried in Arnos Vale cemetery.

JOHN JAMES (1906-1996)

BUSINESSMAN

PLAQUE: PHILIP STREET, BEDMINSTER, BS3 4EA

Ten words on a blue plaque on a farmyard wall sum up John James's attitude to the wealth he built up as a businessman who became a self-made multi-millionaire: 'Philanthropist. Who gave so much to the people of Bristol.'

After leaving the Royal Air Force in 1946 John James, the son of a docker, used his £100 gratuity to open a radio shop and within a year he was running ten stores across the city. Eleven years later he owned what had become the country's largest radio and television retail chain with 300 branches. He sold the business for £6 million. However, this wasn't a signal for John James to sit back and let the grass grow under his feet. Instead, he started up a chain of furniture stores, which he sold in 1979 for £25 million.

His legacy lives on in the endowment he left to the people of Bristol through the John James Bristol Foundation, which was formed in 1983. This charity focuses on supporting education, health services and the elderly. Major donations by the foundation have included more than £1.6 million for magnetic resonance imaging scanners for local hospitals. Another £1.2 million was given to the new Bristol Children's Hospital, which opened in 2001.

A blue plaque marking the life of John James is fixed to the wall of Windmill Hill City Farm, which he financially helped to launch in 1976 by offering £1,000. He promised to continue the offer in the following years. Part of the farm stands on the site of his former birthplace and childhood home in Philip Street. By way of thanks the managers of the farm said that once a year they would give Mr James a cabbage, which had been grown on the spot where he lived.

JAMES JOHNSON (1764-1844)

FOSSIL COLLECTOR

PLAQUE: 12 DOWRY PARADE, BS8 4NQ

James Johnson was one of the country's best-known fossil collectors, and was especially active in searching the rocks of Lyme Regis in Dorset. The Geological Society recorded Johnson as being the first serious collector of fossils in that part of the country, noting him as being active there from the early 1790s onwards. He not only discovered fossils but also bought them.

By the time of his death Johnson's collection of fossils had grown to around 6,000. There were so many that they filled his home in Dowry Parade, Hotwells. Experts regarded the collection as being of such importance that it should be put up for auction.

A year after his death potential buyers – both private and from many museums – packed into Johnson's former home for the sale. The collection was so big that the auction had to be spread over eight days. There was much interest in one particular item, which was listed in the auction catalogue as 'Lot 360'.

This was part of the skull of a huge ichthyosaur, a marine reptile that once ruled the oceans. It had been discovered at Lyme Regis in 1813 and is now held in the Bristol City Museum collection. Johnson had paid £20 for the fossil to be transported from Dorset to his home.

A plaque celebrating Johnson's life was unveiled outside the house where he lived by the Clifton and Hotwells Improvement Society in 2015.

ANNIE KENNEY (1879-1953)

SUFFRAGETTE

PLAQUE: 23 GORDON ROAD, BS8 1AW

Together with Christabel Pankhurst, Annie Kenney was the first suffragette to be imprisoned. They were imprisoned for several days for assault and obstruction after heckling at a Liberal rally discussing votes for women.

Annie, originally a Lancashire mill girl, arrived in Bristol in 1907 because of her work with the suffragette movement. She had been given the responsibility for organising suffragettes in the West of England, becoming the regional organiser for the Women's Social and Political Union (WSPU). She was based in Bristol and paid £2 a week. As part of her job Annie Kenney spoke at, or presided over, scores of public meetings.

In November 1907 a large rally was held at the Victoria Rooms, Clifton, at which Christabel Pankhurst spoke. The following year 10,000 people attended another rally on Clifton and Durdham Downs.

After living in a series of digs in Bristol, Annie Kenney moved into a flat in Gordon Road, Clifton. The inscription on a blue plaque on the front wall of the house describes her as a 'leading suffragette who fought for women's rights'. It says that Annie Kenney lived at the house in 1910. By 1913 she was in charge of WSPU activities in London after Christabel Pankhurst fled to France to avoid arrest.

JOHN LAMBTON, 1st EARL OF DURHAM (1792-1840)

POLITICIAN

PLAQUE: 3 RODNEY PLACE, BS8 4HY

Apart from his medical and scientific interests Dr Thomas Beddoes was also a private tutor. One of his pupils later became a colonial administrator of some note.

John Lambton was placed with Dr Beddoes by his father when he was 6 years old and stayed with him at his home in Clifton for seven years before continuing his education at Eton College.

He went into politics as Member of Parliament for County Durham in the General Election of 1812 holding the seat until 1828, when he was raised to the peerage as Baron Durham.

A number of overseas postings in administrative roles followed, including that of Governor General of British North America.

A plaque outside Dr Beddoes' home in Rodney Place, Clifton, says that Lambton lived there from 1798–1805. The inscription goes on to say that Lambton's 'famous report [on the affairs of British North America] inspired all subsequent British colonial policy'.

The plaque was erected by the Royal Empire Society's Bristol branch and was unveiled in 1933 by the Prime Minister of Canada.

WALTER SAVAGE LANDOR (1775-1864)

WRITER AND POET

PLAQUE: PENROSE COTTAGE, HARLEY PLACE, BS8 3BP

Walter Savage Landor, a doctor's son, was a poet and writer best known for his *Imaginary Conversations*. In this work of prose Landor imagined 150 conversations between the likes of Greek philosophers, contemporary writers and royalty on a variety of topics from politics to romance. Landor's first two editions of *Imaginary Conversations* were published in 1824. They were followed by several more editions over the next five years. Landor also wrote more than 300 poems, many of them in Latin.

Little is known of his short stay in Bristol although it is marked by a plaque on a cottage in Clifton. The inscription says he lived there from 1836–37 before settling in Bath.

SIR ALLEN LANE (1902-1970)

PIONEERING PUBLISHER

PLAQUE:
11 COTHAM VALE. BS6 6HS

Allen Lane, who was born and educated in Bristol, revolutionised the publishing industry. He joined the Bodley Head publishing house as a teenage apprentice and went on to become managing director before leaving the firm to set up Penguin Books.

It is said that Lane came up with the idea for Penguin while waiting at Exeter railway station for a train to London after a meeting with Agatha Christie, the 'queen of thriller writers', at her home in Devon. Lane did not think that the station's bookstall offered anything of quality.

The first book that Lane published under the Penguin imprint was a biography of the poet Shelley by the French writer Andre Maurois. Other early Penguin publications included detective stories by Agatha Christie and Hemmingway's *Farewell to Arms*. To break even Lane needed 17,000 sales on each of his first ten titles, which were being sold at 6*d* each. Within a year more than a million Penguin books had been sold.

In 1960 Lane fought a *cause celebré* with Penguin's publication of an uncensored edition of D.H. Lawrence's controversial book *Lady Chatterley's Lover*. He was prosecuted under the obscenity laws but the charges were dismissed. More than 200,000 copies of the book were sold. Sales were undoubtedly boosted by the publicity from the Old Bailey trial. Even corner shops were asking the publisher for supplies of the book.

He was knighted in 1962 and died in 1970. By then more than 400 million Penguin books had been sold. Lane is far from forgotten in his native city. Its university has a collection of Penguin books signed by the author or editor covering the period 1935–1970. From the early 1970s onwards the university has been sent a copy of each Penguin book published, which works out at about 1m of books a month.

Lane was brought up in a Victorian house in Cotham Vale, just a mile or so north of the centre of Bristol. A blue plaque on the front wall records the time he lived there.

LORD JOHN LAWRENCE (1811-1879)

SIR HENRY LAWRENCE (1806-1857)

PLAQUE: 2 BELLEVUE, BS8 1DA

One of the oldest plaques in the city dates back to 1904. It was unveiled to the memory of Lord John Lawrence and his older brother Sir Henry Lawrence.

Lord Lawrence, who joined the Indian Civil Service, became Viceroy of India for five years from 1864. His brother, a soldier and statesman who held a variety of roles in India, was described by contemporary writers as the 'hero of Lucknow'.

He died aged 51 while defending Lucknow during the Indian Mutiny in 1857. He was injured by an exploding shell and died two days later. Sir Henry is known for establishing four asylums in India for the children of British servicemen. A memorial plaque in St Paul's Cathedral, Kolkata, states that Sir Henry was 'beloved and mourned by natives and Europeans'.

The Clifton Improvement Committee mounted a decorated bronze plaque on the second of a terrace of houses in Bellevue, Clifton, where the brothers once lived. The inscription states that this was the home of their father, Corporal Alexander Lawrence. It goes on to say that the brothers lived there 'in their youth from 1819–1824'.

While they were in Bristol the boys attended the Reverend Gough's Academy for Young Gentlemen on College Green.

SIR THOMAS LAWRENCE (1769-1830)

ARTIST

PLAQUE: 6 REDCROSS STREET. BS2 0BA

Thomas Lawrence's artistic skills first came to light when he was a child drawing pencil sketches of some regular customers in his father's public house. By the time he was 12 years old Lawrence had his own studio and at the age of 18 he moved to London and took lodgings near Sir Joshua Reynolds, who encouraged him to use his studio for studying and copying.

Lawrence soon achieved a great reputation as a portrait painter and exhibited his first full-length portrait two years after arriving in London. He received his first royal commission for a portrait of Queen Charlotte when he was 21.

He became the favourite painter of George III and was eventually appointed Painter in Ordinary to the king. Such was his reputation as a portraitist that he was sent abroad to paint the allied heads of state and generals for the Waterloo Chamber at Windsor Castle. He returned to England in 1820 to find that on that very day he was voted the new president of the Royal Academy.

Lawrence died in London in 1830 never having been short of work. His funeral service took place at St Paul's Cathedral and was something of a national event with sixty-four carriages in the procession.

Thomas Lawrence was born in Redcross Street, Old Market, when his father was landlord of the White Lion Inn, which stood on the site of the present Grand Hotel in Broad Street. By the time he was 12 years old the family had moved to a pub in Bath.

The people of Bristol have a permanent reminder of one of the world's greatest portrait painters in a blue plaque, which identifies his birthplace in Redcross Street, Old Market.

ARCHIBALD LEACH (1904–1986)

FILM ACTOR (CARY GRANT)

PLAQUE: 15 HUGHENDEN ROAD. BS7 8SF

Archibald Alexander Leach could not resist the lure of the footlights, costumes and grease paint of the theatrical world after working behind the scenes at the Bristol Hippodrome. He later went to America with the Bob Pender touring acrobatic group and eventually made his way in Hollywood.

In 1931 he came to the attention of Paramount film studios and signed a contract with them. It was when he was in Hollywood that Archie Leach took on the stagename of Cary Grant.

He made his screen debut in a film called *This Is The Night*, a comedy starring French actress and singer Lili Damita. Over the next three decades Cary Grant starred in seventy-four films including *Arsenic and Old Lace*, *North by Northwest*, *The Philadelphia Story* and *His Girl Friday*. During his career Grant acted with some of the best-known screen stars in the world including Marlene Dietrich, Ingrid Bergman and Audrey Hepburn.

He retired from the silver screen in 1966 after appearing in *Walk Don't Run*, which was set during the Tokyo Olympics. Four years later he was awarded a special Academy Award for his 'unique mastery of the art of screen acting'. He had become a great screen lover and a wonderful comic actor.

Despite his fame Cary Grant never severed his links with his native city. He made frequent visits to his mother Elsie Leach, who lived in a nursing home in Clifton and died in 1973 at the age of 94. He brought each of his five wives to his home city and introduced them to his mother. Grant had a special relationship with a photographer on the local paper whom he alerted about his visits to Bristol. It meant that the paper had a front-page photograph of him ahead of Fleet Street.

Cary Grant was born in a terraced house in Horfield and went to the local Bishop Road Primary School. This was followed by a spell at Fairfield Grammar School from which he was expelled at the age of 14. Some accounts say that this was because he was found in the girls' toilets.

He died in 1986 at the age of 82. His birthplace, a terraced house in Hughenden Road, Horfield, has a blue plaque beside the front door bearing the inscription 'Archie Leach better known as Cary Grant was born in this house'.

VINCENT LEAN (1820-1899)

LAWYER AND BENEFACTOR

PLAQUE: CENTRAL LIBRARY, COLLEGE GREEN, BS1 5TL

The main public library in Bristol at College Green didn't cost the city's ratepayers a penny to build. It was built in the opening years of the twentieth century with the £50,000 that Vincent Lean left in his will for it.

Lean, who had been a barrister and died aged 79 in 1899, stipulated that the money was for 'the further development of the free libraries of the city, and with special reference to the formation and sustentation of a general reference library'. He also bequeathed to the library his collection of about 5,000 books.

The council did Lean proud, setting up a competition to find a designer for the library. It was won by architect Charles Holden. The library was opened in 1905 and with its marble staircase leading from the entrance hall to the first floor the design won national acclaim.

Lean's gift to the city is remembered in a brass plaque at the entrance to the library. The inscription reads: 'This building was bequeathed to the City of Bristol by Vincent Stuckey Lean, A former citizen.'

ADOLPH LEIPNER (1827-1894)

BOTANIST

PLAQUE: 47 HAMPTON PARK, BS6 6LQ

The first botanic garden in Bristol was laid out by Dr Adolph Leipner in 1882 after he had been given a grant of £15 by University College, Bristol, where he was lecturer of botany and zoology. Leipner raised a further £89 and with the total amount he bought more than 500 plants and nearly 250 packets of seeds for the garden. He laid out the garden on what was then wasteland on a corner of Woodland Road, Clifton. Leipner found the garden to be a useful aid in his teaching.

In 1959 the site of Leipner's garden was used to build the University of Bristol's Senate House. The garden, much expanded, is now at Stoke Bishop.

Leipner was born in Germany and moved to London at the age of 20 and lived there for six years before moving to Bristol to teach natural science and German at Clifton College when it opened in 1862. He also lectured on a part-time basis in botany and vegetable physiology at Bristol Medical School. In 1869 he left Clifton College to concentrate on lecturing at the Medical School.

When University College, Bristol, opened its doors in 1876 Leipner was one of its first lecturers. He specialised in botany, zoology and German on a salary of £100 a year which was topped up by two-thirds of the income from his students' fees. When the college was granted full university status in 1909, Leipner was appointed its first professor of botany.

Leipner was a co-founder of Bristol Naturalists' Society which was set up in 1862 and is still going strong more than 150 years later. At the time of his death he was president of the society.

A blue plaque commemorating his work is fixed to the front wall of a house in Redland where he lived from 1870 until his death.

BERTHOLD LUBETKIN (1901–1990)

ARCHITECT

PLAQUE: 113 PRINCESS VICTORIA STREET. BS8 4DD

One of the early projects Russian-born architect Berthold Lubetkin was responsible for in England was described by fellow designers as an 'architectural masterpiece'. This was his modernist Highpoint apartment block built on Highgate Hill, north London.

His design for Highpoint was radical for the time as the apartments included rubbish chutes, which were regarded as innovative, along with tennis courts and a swimming pool. Three years later Lubetkin and his team built a second Highpoint close by. Both apartment blocks, built for private buyers, are now on the government's list of buildings of architectural interest.

Lubetkin was born in Georgia, and studied architecture in Moscow, Berlin and Paris before he moved to London in 1932 and set up his own architectural practice, which he called Tecton. He worked with six students from the Architectural Association in London and pioneered modernist design in Britain.

The first commission for Tecton was to design a gorilla house for London Zoo in Regents Park. Lubetkin was also asked to design buildings for its reserve park at Whipsnade. He was also commissioned to design a completely new zoo at Dudley in the West Midlands, Finsbury Health Centre, and flats at the Spa Green Estate, both in London. The Spa Green flats have been given a Grade II* listing by English Heritage in recognition of its modernist style.

Lubetkin's partnership was dissolved after the Second World War but he himself was appointed architect-planner for one of Britain's new towns – Peterlee, in County Durham. However, not long after being commissioned for this ambitious project, he resigned from it. Lubetkin had become frustrated by bureaucratic intervention by government departments and local authorities.

He virtually retired from architectural work and moved to Gloucestershire, where he became involved in farming. From 1969 until his death in 1990 he lived in Clifton. He campaigned to protect the views of Brunel's Clifton Suspension Bridge, which was close to his home. Lubetkin is commemorated by a large blue circular plaque that has been installed at his former home in Princess Victoria Street by the Design and Industries Association.

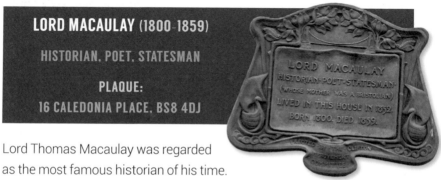

LORD MACAULAY (1800–1859)

HISTORIAN, POET, STATESMAN

PLAQUE:
16 CALEDONIA PLACE, BS8 4DJ

Lord Thomas Macaulay was regarded as the most famous historian of his time.
He is best known for his *History of England from the Accession of James II*. The first two volumes were published in 1848 but the book was in print long

after that because of its popularity. Macaulay was writing the fifth volume of the book at the time of his death. His sister prepared the text for posthumous publication. Macaulay was also known for his essays, reviews and poetry.

In his poem 'Spanish Armada' Macaulay makes special reference to Bristol: 'right sharp and quick, the bells all night rang out from Bristol town, And ere the day three hundred horse had met on Clifton Down.'

Macaulay was also a politician, having been elected as Member of Parliament for Edinburgh. In 1839 he was appointed Secretary of War and in 1846 he became Paymaster General.

A plaque outside a Georgian house in Caledonia Place, Clifton, states that Macaulay lived there in 1852 for his health. It also informs us that his mother was a Bristolian, the daughter of a local bookseller.

JOHN McADAM (1756-1836)

ROAD ENGINEER

PLAQUE: 23 BERKELEY SQUARE. BS8 1HP

The man who gave his name to a revolutionary system of road building that turned rough muddy tracks into smooth surfaces lived and worked in Bristol at the peak of his career.

John Loudon McAdam invented a new way of building roads with a smooth hard surface. His process included using stones that could be graded and laid in three levels, with the smallest stones crushed and laid as a top surface. No stones should be more than 6oz in weight. Later, tar was laid over the top.

McAdam was a Scotsman who in 1816 was appointed General Surveyor of the Bristol Turnpike Trust. He was responsible for 146 miles of roads that the trust covered.

His road-building experiments left him impoverished so he pleaded – in vain – to Bristol Corporation (now city council) for financial help. Later the House of Commons voted him a grant of £2,000. By 1819 the Turnpike Trust controlled 178 miles and McAdam's salary had been increased to £500. Along with his two sons McAdam also worked for a score of other turnpike trusts across the country.

He gave evidence to three parliamentary enquiries on highways, and in 1827 he was appointed surveyor general of metropolitan roads for the whole of England.

McAdam, who became a Freeman of Bristol, in 1811 helped to found and was the first president of the Bristol Commercial Rooms. This was a private club in Corn Street where businessmen met to read the newspapers and discuss commercial affairs of the day with each other. It was the first such club in the city. In its heyday, the Rooms had 1,056 members. However, in 1995, because of dwindling membership, the establishment closed.

While he was in Bristol McAdam lived at several prestigious addresses in Clifton. One of them was an elegant Georgian house in Berkeley Square. A later resident at the house fixed to the exterior wall, at his own expense, a plaque with the inscription that McAdam 'inventor of McAdamised' roads lived here from 1805–1808'.

KASSAM MAJOTHI (1924–2002)

BUSINESSMAN

PLAQUE: ST MARK'S ROAD. BS5 6HX

It's not every shopkeeper who is posthumously honoured with a blue plaque, but then Kassam Majothi was no ordinary retailer.

He was a Ugandan refugee who with his family immigrated to the UK during the reign of Idi Amin, a former president of Uganda who became a ruthless dictator. In 1978 Kassam, with limited funds, opened a small shop selling Indian sweetmeats and home-made foods. No longer is his Bristol Sweet Mart just a local one-off food shop but it has expanded shop by shop down St Mark's Road, Easton, a multicultural inner-city area of Bristol.

Besides Kassam's original shop there is now a delicatessen and a wholesale service. The product range of the business has expanded to include specialist Indian and exotic foods, fresh fruit and vegetables, along with herbs and spices. The retail side of the operation also stocks Polish, Kosovan and Japanese foods. There are now around 10,000 different

Kassam Majothi's Bristol Sweet Mart.

products on the shelves and the firm supplies more than 100 Indian restaurants and cafés in Bristol.

Bristol Sweet Mart is still very much a family-run operation; Kassasm
died in 2002 and his four sons are now at the helm of the business he
set up. Of the fifty or so staff, nearly twenty are from the Majothi family.

When Bristol City Council unveiled the blue plaque in March 2004 at
Kassam Majothi' s original shop, more than 300 people turned up for the
ceremony. The inscription states that he was 'founder of Bristol Sweet Mart'.

FRANK MATCHAM (1854–1920)

THEATRE ARCHITECT

PLAQUE: BRISTOL HIPPODROME. ST AUGUSTINE'S PARADE. BS1 4UZ

Frank Matcham, who was born in Devon the eldest of nine children, became
one of the most prolific theatre designers in Britain. He built or renovated
more than 150 of them all over the country from grand playhouses in
London to suburban and variety theatres.

Matcham took over his late father's architectural practice when he was in his mid-twenties, and spent most of his working life working with theatres.

One that he designed was the Bristol Hippodrome, which opened in 1912 and can seat nearly 2,000 people. One of its features was a specially designed tank underneath the stage which could hold 100,000 gallons of water. It had a hydraulically controlled moving base that was designed to create waves, with the water being heated up to a temperature of 80°F. The tank came into its own on the theatre's opening night in an aqua-drama called the *Sands O'Dee* when the hero of the production galloped on horseback through the water.

Another feature of the Hippodrome's design was the dome in its roof, which is still in place and can be opened to ventilate the building. English Heritage has designated the theatre as a Grade II Listed Building.

The Bristol Hippodrome was the last major theatre built by Matcham. A plaque bearing the simple legend that 'Theatre architect Frank Matcham designed this theatre' has been installed inside the theatre by the Frank Matcham Society. This was not Frank Matcham's first project in the city. He was involved in a revamp of the Prince's Theatre, Park Row, in 1902. The theatre was lost in the Bristol Blitz in 1940.

Frank Matcham died at his home in Essex and is buried in London's Highgate Cemetery. He was 66 years old.

EUGÉNIE MONTIJO (1826–1920)

EMPRESS OF FRANCE

PLAQUE: 3 ROYAL YORK CRESCENT, CLIFTON, BS8 4JW

In 1836 a private school run by a Mrs Rogers and her daughter at their home on Royal York Crescent welcomed two sisters, one of whom was to become Empress of France. Eugénie Montijo and her sister Francisca, who was nicknamed Paca, were enrolled at the boarding school by their father, the Duke of Teba, a Spanish nobleman.

Little is known of their time at the school but the young Eugénie did write to a friend: 'Do not think there are any public amusements here. Everyone stays at home and one never sees a fashionable man in the street.'

Royal York Crescent, where Princess Eugénie was educated.

In a letter dated 'Clifton – July 1837' Paca wrote: 'All day we are indoors learning English'.

After a short stay at Clifton, Eugénie and her sister were taken to Paris to finish their education. Eugénie later met Louis Napoleon, nephew of Napoleon Bonaparte. The couple were married in 1853 and Eugénie became Empress of France.

Her time at Clifton may not have been all that bad for she returned to the area for a couple of days in 1889. She stayed at St Vincent Rocks Hotel close to her old school, which had closed thirty-four years earlier.

Clifton and Hotwells Improvement Society have recorded Eugénie Montijo's time at Clifton with a plaque outside No.3 Royal York Crescent, now residential accommodation.

The crescent itself has its own plaque at its mid-way point telling something of its chequered history. This prestigious crescent of fifty-two houses is said to be the longest in Europe at almost a quarter of a mile long. Work on this development started in 1791 but came to a stand-still two years later. This was at the time of the Napoleonic wars which had caused an economic depression and resulted in the developer going bankrupt. Eight years later the government bought the site along with the unfinished part of the crescent with the intention of building military barracks. However, this plan was thwarted by strong opposition from local people.

Work later resumed on building homes as originally intended and Royal York Crescent was completed in 1820.

HANNAH MORE (1745-1833)

WRITER, PHILANTHROPIST

PLAQUES:
KEEPER'S COTTAGE, 49 BRISLINGTON HILL, BS4 5NJ
4 WINDSOR TERRACE, CLIFTON, BS8 4LW

Hannah More, who was born at Fishponds and was one of five sisters of a schoolmaster, became one of the most influential writers and philanthropists of her time.

She taught at the Academy for Young Ladies in Park Street, which was run by her eldest sisters, and about 1796 she herself started the first school in Brislington. This is now a large suburb of Bristol but at the time was a village in Somerset. Hannah set up her school in Keeper's Cottage, part of the estate belonging to the squire of Brislington.

She was keen to establish herself as a playwright, so moved to London and mixed with people of the theatrical world. She became a talented writer, penning essays, plays, a novel, stories for children, poetry and religious tracts, and was soon accepted by London's bluestocking and literary circles.

She became one of the top-earning writers in eighteenth and nineteenth-century England with an estimated income of £40,000 – equivalent to millions of pounds in today's terms. Hannah left most of her money to religious societies and charities.

However, she gradually turned from writing to social reform, became increasingly religious, fighting poverty, ignorance and drink. She campaigned for the abolition of slavery and helped the poor living in the Mendip villages around Wrington, Somerset, where she had settled with her sisters. She offered educational, spiritual and financial help to miners and agricultural workers. She started Sunday schools in areas of poverty and deprivation.

Living in isolation and suffering from poor health caused Hannah to move to Clifton. She then lived at Windsor Terrace from 1829–1833. Miss More died there aged 88. She was buried with her sisters in Wrington.

Hannah More never married but was engaged three times to the same man who kept postponing their wedding. She reluctantly accepted an annuity from him, which enabled her to live an independent life.

A green plaque given by Clifton and Hotwells Improvement Society is fixed to the house that was Hannah More's home in Clifton and a blue one, which was unveiled by the Lord Mayor, is mounted on the side wall of Keeper's Cottage. It pays tribute to the first school in Brislington.

PROFESSOR CONWY LLOYD MORGAN (1852–1936)

UNIVERSITY ADMINISTRATOR AND ACADEMIC

PLAQUE: 14–16 CANYNGE ROAD, BS8 3JX

Professor Conwy Lloyd Morgan had the distinction of being appointed the first vice chancellor of Bristol University. But he only held the post for a year as he found that the administrative duties involved interfered too seriously with the studies to which he had devoted himself.

Professor Morgan arrived in Bristol in 1884 as professor of zoology at University College. He was appointed principal in 1887 and over the next twenty years played a major role in the campaign to get full university status, which would entitle it to award degrees.

Bristol University was granted its Royal Charter in 1909 and Professor Morgan became its vice chancellor. After resigning that role he continued at the university as professor of philosophy. On his retirement in 1920 he became emeritus professor of psychology and ethics.

Clifton and Hotwells Improvement Society marked Professor Morgan's contribution to the life of the university by unveiling a plaque on the site of the house in Canynge Road, Clifton, in which he lived for seventeen years from 1886. The site at numbers 14–16 Canynge Road is now a block of flats.

WILLIAM JAMES MULLER (1812-1845)
LANDSCAPE ARTIST
PLAQUE: 54-58 WHITE HARTE, PARK ROW, BS1 5LH

It is said that William Muller never retouched a sketch after leaving the place that had inspired it. The Bristol-born landscape artist became known for his watercolours and painted scenes not only of his native city but also from his travels around Europe and Egypt.

He was the son of a Prussian refugee who was appointed the first curator of the Bristol Institution, the forerunner of Bristol Museum. His mother was a Bristolian.

At the age of 15 William was studying under James Baker Pyne, of the Bristol School of Artists, who had a studio in the centre of the city. Muller went on to paint romantic scenes of beauty spots like the Avon Gorge and Leigh Woods.

After a visit to London he exhibited for the first time at the Royal Academy with his work 'Destruction of Old London Bridge – Morning'. He was then 21 years old.

In 1839 Muller based himself in London but later returned to Bristol because of poor health. It's believed that his last days were spent living above the White Harte public house in Park Row, in the centre of Bristol. He died aged 33 and was buried in the Unitarian churchyard in the St Pauls district. A year after his death many of his paintings were put up for sale. Fortunately, some of Muller's works are in the Bristol Museum and Art Gallery.

A square plaque, of unknown origin, can be found on the side wall of the White Harte. It simply states 'W. J. Muller, artist, stayed here'.

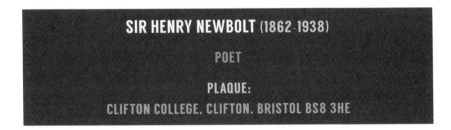

SIR HENRY NEWBOLT (1862–1938)

POET

PLAQUE:
CLIFTON COLLEGE, CLIFTON, BRISTOL BS8 3HE

Some of Sir Henry Newbolt's poetry was inspired by his days at Clifton College, especially the lines: 'There's a breathless hush in the Close tonight / Ten to make and the match to win'. They come from his poem '*Vitaï Lampada*' and the close to which he refers is a playing field outside the college's main buildings where many cricket matches have been played.

The plaque commemorating Sir Henry Newbolt at Clifton College.

Newbolt loved Clifton so much that he wrote the lyrics of the college song 'The Best School of All'; the words of which were later set to music by the composer Sir Hubert Parry.

After arriving at the college as a day boy when he was 14, Newbolt went on to become head boy and later gained a place at Oxford University. After a career in the legal profession as a barrister, Newbolt took to writing, both poetry and prose. Apart from stories for boys he became an authority on naval history and published a book on the encounters of the First World War. In all he wrote twenty-eight books and twelve volumes of his poetry were published.

In 1921 Newbolt wrote a government report entitled 'The Teaching of English in England'. For many years his recommendations were the stand-ard work for English teachers in training colleges.

Newbolt, who died at his home in London aged 75, has been honoured in the grounds of his old college by a plaque, which appropriately stands in a corner of the Close. It was provided by the Clifton and Hotwells Improvement Society with its support frame being made by a former Clifton College pupil.

SIR GEORGE NEWNES (1851–1910)

ENTREPRENEUR. PUBLISHER. POLITICIAN

PLAQUE: SION HILL. CLIFTON. BS8 4LD

The
Clifton Spa Pump Room
Opened 1st August 1894
Architect – Philip Munro (1843–1911)
Built by Sir George Newnes at the
request of the Society of Merchant
Venturers as a place to take the
healing waters and listen to
lunch–time concerts.
DONATED BY
THE CLIFTON AND HOTWELLS
IMPROVEMENT SOCIETY

The plaque on the wall next door to the Avon Gorge Hotel is evocative of a more leisurely era. It tells us that it was on this site that Sir George Newnes built the Clifton Spa Pump Room where people took 'the healing waters and enjoyed lunchtime concerts'. Balls, dinners, tea dances and receptions were also held there.

Sir George, a publisher, Member of Parliament for a Cambridgeshire constituency and an entrepreneur developed the Pump Room and adjoin-ing hotel at the request of the Society of Merchant Venturers, Bristol. The society, which owned much of the land in Clifton, was keen to make it a fashionable spa destination, and Sir George was spurred on by the suc-cess of his funicular railway linking Lynton and Lynmouth in north Devon.

A carving at the entrance to the former Clifton Spa Pump Room.

It seems that no expense was spared on the project. Sir George had two dozen marble pillars erected in the 100ft long Pump Room. He fitted the room out with elaborate plaster cornices and oak furnishings. An arch curving over a spring where Hotwell Spa water bubbled up through the rocks of the Avon Gorge below was the centrepiece of the Pump Room.

Its directors claimed that this was the 'most highly decorated and finest' pump room in the land. The medical director had visited continental spas and baths so that he could bring to Clifton the latest ideas.

The Pump Room was given a civic seal of approval when it was officially opened by the Mayoress of Bristol on 1 August 1894. She was guest of honour at a dinner hosted by Sir George Newnes for several hundred potential patrons. After the obligatory speeches the guests were entertained by the band of the Life Guards with vocals from Madame Strathern, who was described as the 'Queen of Sacred Song'.

By 1922 the popularity of the Pump Room had waned and it was converted into a cinema screening silent films. Six years later the cinema was turned into a ballroom and by the 1960s it had become one of Bristol's most popular dance halls. However, the dancing came to an end in the early 1970s. Since then what remains of the Pump Room has been left to gather cobwebs and the only public reminder of it is the green plaque erected by Clifton and Hotwells Improvement Society on the wall at the start of Sion Hill.

FRANK NORMAN (1930-1980)

NOVELIST AND PLAYWRIGHT

PLAQUE: 155 WHITELADIES ROAD, BS8 2RA

The two words 'author' and 'playwright' on the plaque which supposedly describe his career don't even set the scene for the story of his fascinating and colourful life. No one could guess from looking at the plaque honouring Frank Norman that he was the writer of a book that became a West End hit musical.

Frank Norman was abandoned by his natural parents at an early age and then went through several unsuccessful adoptions. This was followed by spells in various children's homes in the London area. Later there were a number of stints in prison for minor offences that he had committed.

After languishing in a prison cell on the Isle of Wight, Frank Norman decided to turn to a writing career. His first book, appropriately titled *Bang to Rights* (1959), was a memoir about his time in jail. Over the next twenty years or so he wrote a total of nineteen books, some of them autobiographies devoted to a particular time of his life.

Two years after his debut book, Frank saw his *Fings Aint Wot They Used T'Be*, which he had written as a straight play without music, performed on the London stage. It was about cockney lowlife characters in the 1950s. As a musical comedy it was produced by theatre director Joan Littlewood at the Theatre Royal, Stratford East. She asked Lionel Bart to add music and write lyrics for the songs. This turned out to be the start of a professional career for Mr Bart composing pop musicals.

The production transferred to the West End where it became something of a box-office hit running for more than two years, or 886 performances, at the Garrick Theatre. It won the *Evening Standard* award for the best musical in 1960. Its West End cast included the actress Barbara Windsor, who became famous through her appearances in a succession of *Carry On* films. *Fings Ain't Wot They Used T'Be* was so popular that the entertainer Max Bygraves recorded its catchy title song, which went into the record charts.

Altogether Frank wrote four plays, including *Inside Out*, which was about life in prison for a first-time inmate. The curtain went up on this production at the Royal Court Theatre in 1969. However, Norman's literary career was cut short by Hodgkin lymphoma, which claimed his life in 1980 when he was only 50.

Bristol City Council has paid tribute to Frank Norman with a blue plaque although the time that he lived in the city seems to have been fairly short. It was unveiled at his birthplace in Whiteladies Road, Clifton: a large house now given over to a number of firms with offices there. Unfortunately, the plaque, with the minimum of information about Frank, hardly stands out from the nameplates relating to the businesses based in the building.

SIR GEORGE OATLEY (1863-1950)

ARCHITECT

PLAQUE:
BISHOP'S HOUSE, CLIFTON HILL, BS8 1BN

The house with a plaque recalling the time that George Oatley lived there may not be as imposing and certainly not as prominent as the neo-gothic tower he built standing sentinel-like over the centre of Bristol. This landmark is the Wills Memorial Building, which rises 215ft from street level and is the architectural gem of the University of Bristol's campus.

George Oatley designed two spectacular staircases either side of the entrance hall rising up to what is one of the building's best-known public features, the Great Hall. It is here that degree congregations are held twice a year as well as public meetings and the broadcasting of BBC radio programmes. The tower also houses the university's School of Law and School of Earth Sciences.

Oatley crowned the tower with an octagonal belfry which houses Great George, the sixth largest bell in the country, weighing nearly 10 tons.

Construction work on the Wills Memorial Building began in 1914 but was interrupted by the Great War and not completed until 1925. It is said that Oatley's design was inspired by a dream in which he saw a tower on a hall with shields all around it. The building was officially opened by King George V and Queen Mary. Shortly afterwards Oatley was honoured with a knighthood.

The Wills Memorial Building, which stands at the top of Park Street, owes its origin to the brothers Sir George and Mr Henry Herbert Wills, of the tobacco family. They wanted to mark the generosity of their father. Henry Overton Wills had given £100,000 to what was then known as the University College of Bristol, thus enabling it to be granted its Charter in 1909 and become the University of Bristol.

Oatley was a prolific workman who was responsible for much of the present face of Bristol. Among many other buildings, he designed St Edyth's church, Sea Mills, Bristol Homeopathic Hospital, Bristol Baptist College and St Monica's Rest Home at Westbury-on-Trym. He also designed

Bristol University's Wills Memorial Building, designed by George Oatley.

hospitals in other parts of the country including Wiltshire, Lancashire and South Wales.

A plaque at Bishop's House, Clifton Hill, appears to be the only public commemoration of Oatley. It was commissioned by Clifton and Hotwells Improvement Society and states that Oatley lived there from 1902 to 1934. As the building's name suggests, this was the official home of the Bishops of Bristol during the second half of the twentieth century.

WILLIAM PATTERSON (1795–1869)

NAVAL ARCHITECT AND SHIPBUILDER

PLAQUE: ENGINEERS' WALK. ANCHOR ROAD. BS1 5LL

William Patterson, shipbuilder of Wapping Wharf, built the *Great Western* (launched in 1837) and the *Great Britain* (launched in 1843). Both were designed by Brunel, although Patterson designed and built the hull for the *Great Britain*. The *Great Western* was the largest ship in the world at the time.

Probably as a result of his connection with Brunel, Patterson's order book expanded with warships, brigantines, steamers and racing yachts being built at his yard. Unfortunately, disaster struck in 1851 when a wooden-hulled paddle steamship, the *Demerara*, foundered in the River Avon on its maiden voyage to the River Clyde to have engines fitted. Being a canny Scot, Patterson removed the paddles so that the ship could be repaired, converted it into a passenger sailing vessel and renamed it the *British Empire*.

Patterson was born in poverty in Scotland but at 15 years old he was apprenticed to a London shipbuilder, learning the art of building wooden ships and installing early steam engines. He arrived in Bristol when he was 28 years old and soon after owned his own shipyard.

Patterson became a member of the Institute of Naval Architects when it was founded in 1860. Five years later he retired to Liverpool where he died in 1869. His son remained in Bristol to specialise in marine salvage work. William Patterson is remembered by a blue plaque at the engineers' wall of fame in Anchor Road set up by the Retired Professional Engineers Club.

WILLIAM PENNINGTON (1740-1829)

MASTER OF CEREMONIES AT HOTWELLS SPA

PLAQUE: 12 DOWRY SQUARE, HOTWELLS, BS8 4SH

Hotwells Spa attracted many of society's leading lights during its season, which ran from April to September, fitting in quite comfortably with the winter season at the better known spa a dozen miles down the road, at Bath. Among the visitors who flocked to Hotwells seeking a cure for their illnesses by taking the waters were Charles II's queen, Catherine of Braganza, the writer Joseph Addison, the poet William Cowper, playwright Richard Brinsley Sheridan and the founder of the Methodist Church John Wesley.

The existence of a warm spring at the foot of St Vincent's Rocks had long been known but it was not until the seventeenth century that its water was claimed to cure such ailments as kidney diseases, diabetes and scurvy, the latter especially amongst sailors.

In 1795 a local man, William Pennington, was appointed master of ceremonies at the spa. As figurehead of this popular attraction his duties included arranging grand balls, entertainments and other amusements for the visitors. Besides the Pump Room, which overlooked the River Avon, the spa had two large public rooms where breakfast was served and country dances were held under the watchful eye of Mr Pennington.

To make sure that decorum was kept the master of ceremonies drew up the Rules of the Hotwell, an idea later adopted by the spa at Bath. One of the rules instructed that 'a certain row of seats be set apart at the upper end of the room, for ladies of precedence, and foreigners of fashion'.

However, the spa's decline was as fast as its rapid rise after it was discovered that its so-called healing powers may not have been as efficacious as once believed. Many visitors died and were buried in what became known as Strangers' Graveyard on Lower Clifton Hill.

William Pennington lived in Dowry Square, Hotwells, where a plaque marking his life and work was unveiled on his former home – now offices – by the Clifton and Hotwells Improvement Society in 2015. Its inscription says that he held the post of master of ceremonies for thirty years.

He died at the age of 89 and was buried in the vault of Dowry Chapel, almost directly opposite his home. Pennington and his wife, who died the previous year, both had memorial plaques in the chapel but the building no longer exists. It means that the new plaque and The Colonnade, a curved arcade of shops on The Portway once serving the needs of the spa's visitors but now converted into homes, are the only reminders of the heady days of Hotwells Spa.

THE RT REV. JOHN PERCIVAL, BISHOP OF HEREFORD (1834-1918)

HEADMASTER AND CLERGYMAN

PLAQUE: CLIFTON HILL HOUSE, BS8 IBX

When Clifton College opened in September 1862 under the headship of Dr John Percival it had just sixty-nine pupils. On the first day Dr Percival told the students that he wanted to build a school that would turn out boys who would be 'brave, gentlemanly, Christian and classically educated'.

During his sixteen years at the college he became an educational pioneer helping to found University College, Bristol, in 1876. It later became the University of Bristol. He was also instrumental in founding Clifton High School for Girls.

Dr Percival saw Clifton College grow to have 680 pupils and gain the reputation of being one of the best-known public schools in the country. He left the college in 1878 to become president of Trinity College, Oxford. In 1895 he was appointed Bishop of Hereford, a post he held until his death.

It is generally thought that John Percival was the first person to be appointed headmaster of Clifton College but he was, in fact, second choice. The Reverend Charles Evans, a teacher at Rugby, had earlier been appointed to the post but less than a month before Clifton College was due to open he resigned. He had decided to accept the headship of his own old school, King Edward's in Birmingham, instead.

When Percival died aged 84, he was buried according to his own instructions in the vault of the chapel at Clifton College, although this was illegal. The chapel was not licensed for burials.

A plaque on an eighteenth-century Grade II listed house in Lower Clifton Hill says that Percival lived there from 1884–1887. It was then known as Callendar House but it 1911 it was bought by the University of Bristol and incorporated into the neighbouring building, Clifton Hill House, and turned into student accommodation. The text on the plaque describes Percival as an 'educational pioneer'.

SAMUEL PLIMSOLL (1824-1898)

POLITICIAN AND SAFETY AT SEA CAMPAIGNER

PLAQUES:
9 COLSTON PARADE, REDCLIFFE, BS1 6RA
ENGINEERS' WALK, ANCHOR ROAD, BS1 5LL
CAPRICORN QUAY, HOTWELLS ROAD, BS8 4UA

For a man who probably saved countless lives from being lost at sea a plaque high up on his birthplace where it can hardly be seen doesn't seem to do justice to him.

Samuel Plimsoll, who earned the sobriquet the Seaman's Friend, had various jobs before coming to public notice as a politician. He worked in a solicitor's office, managed a brewery, was secretary of the Sheffield Committee of the Great Exhibition 1851 and even became a coal merchant.

Plimsoll was elected as Member of Parliament for Derby in 1868. As a politician he passionately campaigned for improvements in safety standards on cargo ships. He published a book *Our Seamen* in which he made allegations about 'unscrupulous' ship owners. Plimsoll ensured that every Member of Parliament had a copy, especially as many of them were ship owners.

He expressed his concern about the number of seamen who were losing their lives at sea because of overloaded cargo ships. According to Hansard, the official record of the House of Commons, on one occasion Plimsoll referred to ship owners as having 'murderous tendencies'. He claimed that they had frustrated and talked to death any effort to procure a remedy for this'. In an angry mood he even shook his fist at the Speaker of the House.

Plimsoll's doggedness eventually led to the passing of the Merchant Shipping Act of 1876. It became obligatory for the owner of every British ship to have a load line painted on each side of the vessel. This took the shape of a disc 1ft in diameter with a horizontal line 18in long drawn through its centre. It became known as the Plimsoll Line.

Besides the plaque on the site of Plimsoll's birthplace in Colston Parade, Redcliffe, erected by the Bristol Society of Merchant Venturers, there is a blue one on the engineers' wall of fame in Anchor Road, which was installed by the Retired Professional Engineers' Club. Another plaque is fixed to the base of a plinth, which supports a marble bust of Plimsoll. Fittingly, he is facing the water of Bristol's harbourside and Brunel's restored SS *Great Britain*.

CECIL POWELL (1903–1969)

PHYSICIST, NOBEL LAUREATE

PLAQUE: 12 GOLDNEY AVENUE, BS8 4RA

Cecil Frank Powell was a relatively unknown physicist when he discovered a new particle – the pion – in cosmic radiation. But this breakthrough in science put him on the road to international fame. He was elected a fellow of the Royal Society in 1949; in 1950, three years after his discovery, Powell was awarded the Nobel Prize for Physics. He became president of the World Federation of Scientific Workers in 1956.

Powell called for international collaboration in science and played a major role in the establishment of the European Organization for Nuclear Research (CERN), based in Geneva. By this point he had become a highly respected figure in the international scientific community.

His career started a year after he was awarded his doctor of philosophy degree in physics in 1927. Powell joined the newly opened Wills Physics Laboratory at Bristol University as a research assistant and spent the rest of his career at the university, subsequently becoming a lecturer, then reader and from 1948–63 the Melville Wills professor of physics, Henry Overton Wills professor of physics and director of the physics laboratory.

During a busy work schedule Powell advised the government on nuclear weapons and took part in an expedition to the West Indies while studying volcanic activity. He was also a scientific advisor to the philosopher Bertrand Russell.

Cecil Powell, who wrote a number of papers relating to physics, died just eight days after his retirement while walking in the Alps whilst staying with friends in Italy.

A commemorative plaque donated by the Clifton and Hotwells Improvement Society to celebrate his career is mounted on the house in Goldney Avenue, Clifton, which was Powell's home from 1954 until his death in 1969.

JAMES COWLES PRITCHARD (1786-1848)

PHYSICIAN AND ETHNOLOGIST

PLAQUE: RED LODGE MUSEUM, PARK ROW, BS1 5LJ

James Pritchard, who became an eminent ethnologist, studied medicine in Bristol, although he graduated in Edinburgh. In 1811 he became physician at St Peter's Hospital and later was appointed physician at Bristol Infirmary, a post he held for many years. Pritchard was responsible for much pioneering work with medical studies in the city.

At the same time as pursuing his medical career Pritchard became fascinated by ethnology and wrote several books on the subject. He published *Researches into the Physical History of Man* and followed it up with his *Treatise on Insanity*, which was long considered to be the standard work on this branch of medical science. Pritchard was also the author of *The Eastern Origin of the Celtic Nations* and *The Natural History of Man*, the latter foreshadowing the work of naturalist Charles Darwin.

A plaque of unknown origin at the entrance to what is now the Red Lodge museum on Park Row states that Pritchard lived there from 1827–45. He died in London at the age of 62.

THOMAS PROCTOR (1811-1876)

BUSINESSMAN AND BENEFACTOR

PLAQUE: ST MARY REDCLIFFE CHURCH. BS1 6RA

A brass plaque in St Mary Redcliffe church pays tribute to one of its benefactors but his identity was a secret for more than twenty years.

The plaque honours Thomas Proctor who was churchwarden at Redcliffe when the appeal fund for the church's third great restoration (1846–77) was launched. He told the vicar of the day that he had received a letter from a donor offering to pay the whole cost of £2,600 for restoring the North Porch of the church. But the offer was conditional in that no attempt should be made to discover the identity of the donor and that the letter was not shown to anyone. It was signed *Nil Desperandum* (Despair of Nothing).

As a guarantee of good faith the writer included £20 to pay for the architect's drawing and estimates. The donor also requested that a reply to his proposition should appear in a local newspaper. The publicity this received spurred on many more people to contribute to the restoration fund.

After Thomas Proctor died in 1876 it was revealed that he himself was *Nil Desperandum*. In addition to his initial gift Proctor made other frequent donations under that guise. He had become wealthy through his chemical, manure and fertiliser business and his dealings in property.

The inscription on the plaque says that Proctor not only repaired the North Porch but 'greatly encouraged the work'.

EÇA DE QUERIOZ (1845-1900)

PORTUGUESE CONSUL AND NOVELIST

PLAQUE: 38 STOKE HILL. BS9 1EX

A plaque on the gate post of a house on Stoke Hill pays tribute to a novelist whose work is not widely known in this country, if at all. But in his native Portugal, Eça de Querioz held a honoured place in literature, comparable to that of Charles Dickens in England.

Eça de Querioz came to England as the Portugese consul based in Bristol and it is said that while he was in the city he produced some of his best writing.

A contemporary critic wrote of him: 'He castigated with caustic and mordant wit, and dissected without pity with the fine scalpel of acute criticism the vices, the inconsistencies, the grotesque manners, the ridiculous customs and the moral deformities of the Portuguese bourgeoisie.'

While in Bristol he lived in a house on Stoke Hill, which was unusual in that it was built on an artificial slope with a wine cellar underneath the terrace.

The plaque describes Eça de Querioz as a 'Portuguese novelist' and says that he was 'Consul in Bristol 1878–1888'. It was unveiled in 1960 by the Portuguese ambassador to England.

CANON HARDWICKE RAWNSLEY (1851-1920)

CLERGYMAN AND CONSERVATIONIST

PLAQUE: 82 ASHLEY ROAD, BS6 5NT

One of the co-founders of the National Trust was Canon Hardwicke Rawnsley who started his Church career in Bristol.

Hardwicke Rawnsley arrived in Bristol in 1875 and was the first curate of Clifton College Mission, which was attached to St Barnabas church based in the impoverished area of St Pauls. At the time he described the area as 'muck heaps and farm refuse, on which jerry builders had set up rows of houses, which periodically got flooded and sucked up fever and death from chill for the poor folk who lived there,' adding that it possessed 'a few public houses of the worst sort.'

Besides holding Sunday services Mr Rawnsley set up a club for working men and played football with teenage boys and took them on walks.

Canon Rawnsley moved from Bristol in 1878 to the Lake District to become the vicar of Lower Wray, near Windermere. At the same time he worked passionately for the protection of England's natural countryside, coastline and historic buildings. This led him to become a co-founder of the National Trust, which was launched in July 1894. His co-founders were two other philanthropists – Octavia Hill and Sir Robert Hunter. It had become essential, they said, to form an association that could not only save the nation's treasures but also hold and look after them.

Canon Rawnsley also found time to write more than forty books, some on religious subjects and others about the Lake District.

When Canon Rawnsley died, the writer of his obituary in *The Times* said of him: 'It is no exaggeration to say – and it is much to say of anyone – that England would be a much duller and less healthy and happy country if he had not lived and worked.'

A cast-aluminium plaque designed by local artist Mike Baker commemorates Canon Rawnsley's life. It features a portrait of him along with scenes depicting his time in both Bristol and the Lake District. When the Lord Mayor unveiled it he was joined by representatives of the National Trust. The plaque can be seen on the wall of the Community of the Sisters of the Church in Ashley Road, St Pauls, close to the site of St Barnabas church, which was demolished in 1983.

SIR MICHAEL REDGRAVE (1908-1985)

ACTOR

PLAQUE: HORFIELD ROAD, ST. MICHAEL'S HILL, BS2 8EA

It is said that Michael Redgrave was given his first name because his mother could see the tower of the church of St Michael on the Mount Without from her maternity bed. Her son was born above a newsagent's shop on Horfield Road in the St Michael parish.

Redgrave was educated at Clifton College, whose theatre was later named after him, before going on to Cambridge University. He started his stage career in repertory at the Liverpool Playhouse and spent two years with the Liverpool Repertory Company.

He went on to become the star of films including *The Lady Vanishes*, *The Sea Shall Not have Them* and *The Dam Busters*. On the stage he made a name for himself with classical roles such as Hamlet, Richard II and Uncle Vanya.

Redgrave, who was knighted for his services to the theatre, died in 1985 at the age of 77. He was survived by his wife and their three children, who all went into the acting profession. His son Corin attended the unveiling of a blue plaque celebrating Sir Michael's life, which is mounted on the former newspaper shop in Horfield Road off St Michael's Hill.

JEREMY REES (1937-2003)

ARTS ADMINISTRATOR

PLAQUE: 20 CANYNGE SQUARE. BS8 3LA

Little could Jeremy Rees have imagined that the arts centre he set up in some empty rooms above a bookshop would later attract national attention.

It was in 1961 that Rees with his wife, Annabel Lawson, and the painter John Orsborn took a fourteen-year lease on the first-floor rooms in Clifton, close to Bristol's civic-run art gallery and the Royal West of England Art Academy. Each of the three founders of the Arnolfini Centre for Contemporary Arts, as Rees called his gallery, put up £100. Annabel and John Orsborn staffed the gallery for two years without payment. Jeremy Rees became the part-time director, also unpaid.

In its early years the Arnolfini attracted solo exhibitions by the likes of artist Gillian Ayres, painter and sculptor Peter Lanyon and painter Alana Davie. There were also group shows of British printmaking, new British sculpture – with exhibits in the open air around Bristol – and displays of contemporary jewellery.

Rees pioneered business sponsorship, gallery sales of prints and paintings, picture loan schemes and education and outreach activities. From the Arnolfini's early days there was a programme of musical events, performance, readings and films. Rees was always keen to experiment with new departures in the arts and started a gallery collection of artists' videos.

New investment funding in 1968 from supporters and an Arts Council grant meant that Rees could become a full-time director. In 1975 the Arnolfini moved into a former dockside warehouse on Bristol's Narrow Quay. Ever since then this has been its permanent home. The larger space meant that Rees was able to expand the music, dance and film programmes. A cinema, restaurant and bar were also added.

Rees continued to direct the Arnolfini until 1986 when he left to work as an arts management consultant. He later became interested in the uses of information technology in museums and libraries, and in problems of intellectual copyright in the electronic media, writing and speaking fields.

He died in 2003 aged 66 in a traffic accident in London. Obituaries in the national newspapers described him as 'a visionary arts administrator' and said that he 'was way ahead of his time'.

The arts centre's unusual name came from a visit that Rees made to the National Gallery where he saw Jan Van Eyck's famous portrait 'The Marriage of the Arnolfini', a full length double portrait in oil of an Italian merchant, believed to be Giovanni Arnolfini with his bride. A blue plaque on a house in Canynge Square, Clifton, states that Rees 'lived here from 1961–1989'.

CHARLES RICHARDSON (1814-1896)

CIVIL ENGINEER

PLAQUES:
ANCHOR ROAD. BS1 5LL
8-10 BERKELEY SQUARE. BS8 1HH

He may not be as famous as his employer but the work that Charles Richardson did was just as important. From an early age Richardson showed an interest in engineering and at 19 he became apprenticed to the great Victorian engineer Isambard Kingdom Brunel. Three years later Brunel, recognising his talent, appointed Richardson to supervise numerous railway-building projects in Bristol and Gloucestershire.

But Richardson's great achievement was building the railway tunnel underneath the Severn Estuary for the Bristol and South Wales Union Railway. This was a massive project about 50ft underneath the seabed and 4½ miles long. However, Richardson, whose idea this was, remained undaunted. The tunnel runs from South Gloucestershire to Monmouth in South Wales.

It took thirteen years to complete the tunnel, which is lined with some 75 million bricks. Some of them were made by the Cattybrook

Brick Company in South Gloucestershire while others came mainly from brickworks in Bristol and Staffordshire. Richardson himself had founded the Cattybrook company which he set up at Cattybrook in South Gloucestershire. Apparently he was impressed by the standard of clay found in the area.

Richardson died aged 81, a week after a paralytic seizure, but is remembered by two plaques in Bristol. A blue one was unveiled in 2014 by the Retired Professional Engineers' Club, Bristol, on their gallery of engineering fame in Anchor Road. The following year the Clifton and Hotwells Improvement Society fixed a green plaque to the house in which he lived in Berkeley Square, Clifton, when he was working on the tunnel.

GENERAL SIR ABRAHAM ROBERTS (1784–1873)

INDIAN ARMY GENERAL

· PLAQUE: 23 ROYAL YORK CRESCENT, CLIFTON, BS8 4JX

A late nineteenth-century directory shows that Royal York Crescent, Clifton, was a popular address with titled people, clergymen, surgeons and servicemen. The latter included a general, a captain and a colonel. The prestigious crescent, with its balconied houses, was the home of one of Britain's great generals, Sir Abraham Roberts, who joined the East India Company, fought in the first Afghan war and served in India for nearly fifty years.

He was invested with one of the country's top honours as a Knight Grand Cross of the Order of the Bath.

An impressive black plaque with an engraving of the nearby Clifton Suspension Bridge was placed outside his home by the long defunct Clifton Improvement Committee. It states that Lord Roberts 'a distinguished Indian General lived in this house for many years and died here'. It also states that General Roberts's son, field marshal the 1st Earl Roberts, who served in the British Army for fifty-three years and was awarded the Victoria Cross, also lived in the house in his early life. He returned to Clifton to unveil the bronze plaque, which had been installed at the beginning of the twentieth century.

CAPTAIN WOODES ROGERS (1679-1732)

PRIVATEER AND COLONIAL GOVERNOR

PLAQUE: 35 QUEEN SQUARE, BS1 4LU

Captain Woodes Rogers gained fame as the commander of a privateering expedition around the world which started in 1708 and lasted three years. For the expedition two merchant ships, the *Duke* and the *Duchess,* were fitted out and set sail from Avonmouth.

Not long into the voyage, Woodes Rogers, who was on board the *Duke,* suppressed a mutiny. Various ships with their cargoes were captured during the expedition and towns were taken and held to ransom.

Rogers is mainly remembered for rescuing the Scots sailor, Alexander Selkirk, who had been marooned on the island of Juan Fernandez in the South Pacific Ocean. He brought him back to Bristol where tradition has it Selkirk met the author Daniel Defoe in the Llandoger Trow pub and became the inspiration for his novel *Robinson Crusoe.* Woodes Rogers also wrote his own journal about his expedition, which he called *A Cruising Voyage Round The World.*

In 1718 Woodes Rogers, who had been made a freeman of Bristol, was appointed the first captain general and governor-in-chief of the Bahama Islands by King George. Since Charles II's time the Bahamas had been under British sovereignty but without any effective Crown government. Woodes Rogers held that office for two separate spells making it his policy to rid the islands of thousands of pirates with bribes, punitive action and pardoning. The Bahamas lay close to busy trade routes for ships carrying everything from rum and other tropical goods to the treasures of Mexico and Peru.

Woodes Rogers died in Nausau and was buried there. A plaque on an office block in Queen Square describes him as a 'great seaman, navigator, colonial governor'.

ISAAC ROSENBERG (1890–1918)

POET

PLAQUE: 25 GARAMOUND HOUSE, CLARENCE ROAD, BS1 6RP

He may not be as well known as the war poets Rupert Brooke, Wilfred Owen or Siegfried Sassoon but Isaac Rosenberg is Bristol's very own First World War poet. Indeed, Sassoon praised his genius and T.S. Eliot called him the 'most extraordinary of the Great War poets'.

Rosenberg was born in the slums of Adelaide Place, not far from St Mary Redcliffe church with its cloud-piercing spire standing sentinel-like over his childhood home. He was the son of Lithuanian Jews who had emigrated from Russia so that his father could avoid military service. For the first seven years of Rosenberg's life his family lived in Redcliffe. They then moved to the East End of London to be part of a Jewish community. Rosenberg's father became a market trader there.

Rosenberg left school when he was 14 years old and became an apprentice engraver in London. Wealthy patrons from a Jewish family paid for him to study at the Slade School of Art, where his love of art and poetry was encouraged.

When war broke out he enlisted with the army and was sent to the Somme on the Western Front in France. Rosenberg, who was against war from the start, was killed in one of the Germans' last offensives of the war on 1 April 1918.

While he was in the confined spaces of the trenches Rosenberg wrote poetry on scraps of paper which he managed to send home to be typed. His *Poems from the Trenches* were published as a collection after the war. Rosenberg's name, along with those of other noted First World War poets, is carved on a stone in Poets' Corner at Westminster Abbey.

In Redcliffe he is remembered by a blue plaque mounted on a nondescript block of flats in Commercial Road known as Garamound House. These flats are near the site of Rosenberg's birthplace, which has long been demolished.

SIR ARCHIBALD RUSSELL (1904-1995)

DESIGNER OF CONCORDE

PLAQUES:
GLENDOWER HOUSE, CLIFTON PARK, BS8 3BP
ENGINEERS' WALK ANCHOR ROAD, BS1 5LL

Sir Archibald Russell, the British designer of Concorde, wanted to be an engineer from about 6 or 7 years of age. He once said that he could never get enough Meccano sets to play with.

At Bristol University Russell qualified as an automobile engineer and got his first job with the Bristol Omnibus Company. He later described his work with the firm as 'overhauling buses'. In 1926 he moved to the Bristol Aeroplane Company as an assistant stress calculator. This was at a time when the firm was still building biplanes.

Russell was involved in the design of the Second World War bombers, the Blenheim and the Beaufort. He was promoted to chief engineer and was responsible for the Brabazon, at the time the world's biggest aircraft. It made its maiden flight from the aircraft factory at Filton in 1949 but four years later the government scrapped the plane, which had never flown commercially.

Russell retired in 1969, shortly after Concorde's maiden flight from the Filton airfield. He was then chairman of the Filton Division of the British Aircraft Corporation, following the merger of the Bristol Aeroplane Company. He was knighted the following year.

A plaque marking his career was fixed to the front of the house in which he had lived by the Clifton and Hotwells Improvement Society. It was unveiled in 2012 by his wife and son. The plaque is sited close to the window where Sir Archibald sat writing his memoirs. He is also honoured by a blue plaque on the Retired Professional Engineers' Club wall of engineering fame in Anchor Road.

RONALD RUSSELL (1910-1994) AND PEGGY ANN WOOD (1912-1998)

THEATRE PRODUCERS

PLAQUE: COLSTON HALL. COLSTON STREET. BS1 5AR

A blue plaque inside the Colston Hall marks the heyday of repertory theatre in Bristol. It is dedicated to husband and wife team Ronald Russell and his wife Peggy Ann Wood, who ran the Rapier Players weekly repertory theatre company continuously for twenty-eight years.

The couple presented more than 900 productions – nearly fifty were world premieres – from the works of Strindberg to Noel Coward and Terrence Rattigan.

The Rapier Players kept going without any local or central government subsidy. Productions were even staged during the Second World War without stop. While Ronald served in the Police War Reserves his wife ran the theatre company single-handedly. The gruelling schedule meant that the theatre company were in rehearsal all day, then on stage at night and at weekends for matinees.

The theatre company was a story in itself. It was based in the Little Theatre, which could seat an audience of 450 inside the Colston Hall. When the Colston Hall burnt down in 1945 the Rapier Players lost all their records, props and costumes but were back on stage within a week.

Ronald and Peggy Ann ran the Rapier Players from 1935–63, when the Little Theatre was taken over by the subsidised Bristol Old Vic Theatre Company.

The plaque, which says that the home of the Rapier Players was 'here at the Little Theatre', was unveiled in 2002 by actor Timothy West, who had appeared in some of the Rapier Players' productions and produced others.

BERTA SACOF (1899-1989), HELEN BLOOM (1901-1987) AND JEANNETTE BRITTON (1910-1991)

POLITICAL AND COMMUNITY ACTIVISTS

PLAQUE: 8 CRANBROOK ROAD, REDLAND, BS6 7BN

When members of the Bristol Civic Society erected their first blue plaque after taking over administration of the scheme from the city council, they invited the Lord Mayor to unveil it

A goodly crowd of family, friends, and society members gathered for the unveiling ceremony outside a house in Redland in Autumn 2015. It was here that the sisters Berta Sacof, Helen Bloom and Jeannette Britton (née Strimer) lived. Their father was a snuff merchant. From their forties onwards it seems that the sisters led lives of tireless political and community activity. For a while all three sisters were Bristol City Councillors at the same time.

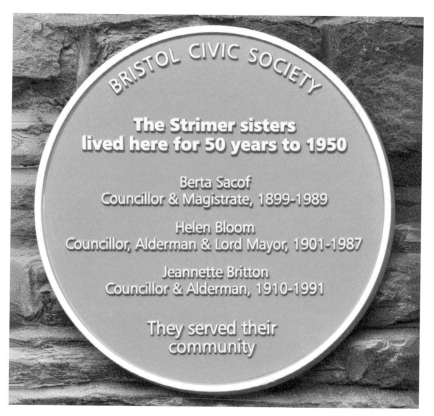

In 1971 Helen Bloom was elected by her fellow councillors as Lord Mayor of Bristol. She was only the third woman to hold the prestigious office although there had been mayors and Lord Mayors in the city since 1216. The other two sisters became aldermen. Between them the three sisters played a major role in shaping twentieth-century life in Bristol in everything from health and education to criminal justice.

The plaque carries the legend 'They served their community'.

ARTHUR (ART) EDWARD SATHERLEY (1889–1986)

RECORD PRODUCER

PLAQUE: CORNER OF BARTLEY STREET/PHILIP STREET. BS3 4EA

It may be that country music is rooted more in Bristol than in Nashville, Tennessee. For it was Bristolian Arthur (better known as Uncle Art) Satherley who discovered many of the American country stars who have since become household names.

When he was inducted into America's Country Music Hall of Fame in 1972 – the first British person to be so honoured – Johnny Cash told the audience: 'If it wasn't for Uncle Art none of us would be on stage.' He added: 'Uncle Art, we owe you everything. He is the daddy of us all.' This was a reference to Satherley 'discovering' many American blues and country music artists.

Arthur Edward Satherley was born and brought up in Bedminster and educated at Queen Elizabeth's Hospital. During his childhood he was fascinated by tales of cowboys and life in the American Wild West. In 1913 he sailed by steamer from Avonmouth Docks across the Atlantic and eventually found work with the Wisconsin Chair Company, making cabinets for Thomas Edison's early phonographs. Satherley worked as a secretary for Edison before moving to Paramount Records, where he was artist and repertoire director. It was his job to find and sign up new talent.

Satherley later moved to Columbia Records and recorded many artists including Gene Autry, Carl Smith and Hank Penny. He also recorded King Oliver's Band, which included a young Louis Armstrong. Satherley retired to California, where he died in 1986.

The cottage in which Satherley was born has long been demolished and replaced by industrial units. A blue plaque honouring him was therefore erected on a building close to his birthplace on the corner of Bartley Street and Philip Street in 2013. The inscription on the plaque, which was unveiled by the Lord Mayor, describes Satherley as a 'pioneering talent scout and record producer'. It also bears an extract from Johnny Cash's speech at the Country Music Hall of Fame in 1972.

EMMA SAUNDERS (1841-1927)

CHARITY WORKER

PLAQUE: TEMPLE MEADS RAILWAY STATION. BS1 6QF

About one million travellers use one of the West Country's largest railway stations each year but few take the time to look at an elaborate marble plaque at the entrance. It is a feature of Temple Meads station which was installed in memory of Emma Saunders, who was known as 'the Railwaymen's Friend'.

Most days she walked from her home on Sion Hill in Clifton to the station carrying a basket of posies, which she gave to the men either to wear as buttonholes or to take home. She also handed out bags of lavender and religious tracts. Emma often visited the sick at their homes and also took it upon herself to give families news of railway accidents.

The Great Western Railway gave Miss Saunders a metal pass which allowed her to travel on any train in the Bristol area so that she could visit men working at outlying stations, wagon sheds or carting depots. She was also a familiar face on the Harbour Railway that linked the City Docks with Temple Meads station.

Miss Saunders also set up the Bristol and West of England Railwaymen's Institute, providing rail workers with teetotal canteens and leisure activities including billiards, skittles and bagatelle. Religious meetings were also organised.

Emma was so loved by the railwaymen that 5,000 of them contributed to an armchair and settee for her home as an 80th birthday gift. When she died, rail workers shouldered her coffin from her home to Christ Church, Clifton, for the funeral service. The church was packed with hundreds of railwaymen, all wearing a buttonhole daffodil which was Emma's favourite flower.

Bristol Temple Meads railway station.

The memorial plaque at Temple Meads depicts Miss Saunders carrying a basket of flowers in one hand and a pamphlet in the other. It was unveiled at a special ceremony with the Great Western Locomotive choir providing musical accompaniment. The inscription says the plaque was erected by railwaymen and friends 'in grateful remembrance of her fifty years devoted Christian service'.

RICHARD SAVAGE (1697-1743)

POET AND PLAYWRIGHT

PLAQUE: GALLERIES SHOPPING CENTRE, BS1 3XE

It could be said that Bristol has seen more than its fair share of colourful and curious characters. Richard Savage, the poet and playwright, was one of them. He lived for a short time in the city in the eighteenth century.

He put himself forward as Poet Laureate but was turned down. As a consolation Queen Caroline gave him a pension of £50 a year on condition that he wrote an ode to mark her birthday each year. Savage styled himself as the Volunteer Laureate. The pension, which he apparently squandered on debauchery, was withdrawn on Queen Caroline's death and he turned to friends for financial support.

History tells us that Savage led a dissipated life and was involved in a fatal brawl in a Charing Cross coffee shop that led to him appearing before a Grand Jury at the Old Bailey. He was found guilty of murder and was condemned to death. Three months later he was given a royal pardon.

Little seems to be known of the time Savage spent in Bristol, save that in January 1743 he was arrested for non-payment of a debt of £8 to a woman and was committed to the city's Newgate Prison. He died there seven months later and was buried the next day at the expense of the prison's gaoler at St Peter's church, the nearest place of religious worship.

Dr Johnson, who wrote a biography of Savage, says that he was writing poems right up until his death. At least one of Savage's plays was staged at the Theatre Royal in King Street.

A memorial plaque on the site of Newgate Prison, now the Galleries Shopping Centre, records the time he languished there awaiting execution.

REVEREND PROFESSOR ARCHIBALD SAYCE (1845-1933)

ASSYRIOLOGIST

PLAQUE: CLIFTON HILL HOUSE, LOWER CLIFTON HILL, BS8 1BX

Although he suffered poor health as a child, Archibald Sayce was a voracious reader and by the age of 10 he was studying Virgil. He eventually went to Oxford University to read Classics. He was later appointed professor of Assyriology at the university, holding the chair from 1891 to 1919.

Sayce was fascinated by the history of the ancient Mesopotamian civilisations and learnt to write in various ancient and modern languages. He wrote nearly fifty papers and books, mainly on Assyriology. They included the first grammar in English of Assyrian, a history of the Hebrews, and books about the people of the region and their literature. He was also a member of the Old Testament Revision Company and wrote extensively on biblical criticism.

Archibald Sayce was born in Shirehampton, Bristol, the son of a clergyman. He is remembered by a plaque at Clifton Hill House, where he lived from 1851–53. He died in Bath aged 86.

In his will he left his notes and collections of antiquities from the Middle and Far East to various learned organisations and institutions including the Ashmolean Museum, Oxford.

ELLEN (1769-1849), JAMES (C. 1751-1811) AND ROLINDA SHARPLES (1793-1838)

ARTISTS

PLAQUE: 37 CANYNGE ROAD, BS8 3LD

Clifton and Hotwells

ELLEN SHARPLES
(1769-1849)
and
ROLINDA SHARPLES
(1793-1838)
MOTHER AND DAUGHTER
ARTISTS
LIVED HERE
1821-1832
Improvement Society

The Sharples family set up something of a cottage industry using their artistic skills. For every portrait of an eminent person that James Sharples painted from life his wife Ellen copied it. The likenesses were so good that they were shown in public art galleries or sold.

Among the famous people that Sharples painted were the Bristol-born Poet Laureate Robert Southey, the scientist Sir Humphrey Davy, the Count of Beaujolais and the French diplomat Talleyrand.

When the Sharples moved to America, James painted a portrait of the country's first president, George Washington. Remarkably, thirty-six copies were made. He also painted a profile of Washington's wife, Martha.

The Sharples stayed in America until James died in 1811 and Ellen, who was born in Bath, returned to England with her family. They settled in Bristol and Ellen brought up daughter Rolinda to be a professional artist. Rolinda is probably best known for her scenes of Bristol's social life in the nineteenth century. She was one of the first British women artists to tackle multi-figure compositions. They included the popular annual horse races on Durdham Downs and the cloakroom at the Assembly Rooms in Clifton. Rolinda's life was, unfortunately, cut short at the age of 44 by cancer.

Four years before Ellen Sharples died she gave £2,000 towards the cost of building Bristol's first fine art academy. In her will she bequeathed another £3,645 as well as nearly 100 pictures towards the cost of building and setting up the academy. Her donations, along with other financial gifts from art lovers, meant that work could start on building the academy, which opened in 1858. Mrs Sharples' pictures formed the beginnings of its permanent collection. Patrons of the academy in its early days included the engineer Isambard Kingdom Brunel.

The building was considerably altered in 1911 when two flights of steps either side of the main entrance were removed. A new foyer was constructed and the building extended. Today the academy, now known as the Royal West of England Academy of Art, has the distinction of being one of only five royal academies in the United Kingdom. Its patron is the queen.

When the Sharples' returned to England from America they lived at various addresses in Bristol including St Vincent's Parade in Hotwells, and Sion Spring House in Clifton. However, it was at an imposing semi-detached four-storey house in Canynge Road, Clifton, that the city's high sheriff unveiled a green plaque in 2003 commemorating Ellen and Rolinda Sharples. Erected by the Clifton and Hotwells Improvement Society at the gateway of the house, it records that 'mother and daughter, artists, lived here 1821–1832'.

FIELD MARSHAL VISCOUNT WILLIAM SLIM OF BURMA (1891-1970)

MILITARY COMMANDER

PLAQUES:
COLSTON AVENUE. BS1 1EB
72 BELMONT ROAD. BISHOPSTON. BS6 5AT

The top brass of the British Army regarded Bill Slim as 'the finest general that the Second World War produced'; his troops affectionately called him Uncle Bill.

This son of a travelling hardware salesman joined the army at the start of the First World War and served in Gallipoli and Mesopotamia. Much of his military career, though, was spent in India and when the Second World War broke out he was sent to head the Burma campaign, leading the famous 14th 'Forgotten Army' to victory over the Japanese.

Slim was in command of more than a million British and Commonwealth troops. This was Britain's most diverse and largest ever army unit. It comprised men from twenty-eight nationalities and of many cultures and beliefs. Slim had even learned to speak the native tongue of many of his soldiers. Back at home, though, his troops became known as the 'Forgotten Army' because most attention was paid to the war in Europe and North Africa.

When the war ended Slim was made head of the Imperial General Staff, Britain's top military post. In 1953 he was appointed Governor General of Australia, a role he held for seven years.

William Slim was born in Bishopston, where a blue plaque has been fixed to the front wall of his birthplace. The inscription describes him as a 'great military commander'. He died in London in 1979 at the age of 88.

In 2008 several hundred people, including old soldiers and their families from many communities in Bristol, gathered in the city centre to witness Bill Slim's son – the Second Viscount Slim – unveil a bronze plaque dedicated to the '14th Army 1942–45'.

Measuring more than 2ft in diameter and set in a stone plinth close to the Cenotaph on Colston Avenue, it bears an inscription which, in part, says: 'Field Marshal Sir William ("Uncle Bill") Slim, the 1st Viscount of Bishopston and Yarramulla, KG, GCB, CCMG, GCVO, CBE, DSO, MC led the army that defeated the Japanese invasion of India in 1944 and Liberated Burma in 1945.' The text goes on to say that 'the men and women of the Fourteenth Army fought for the cause of freedom'.

The plaque, which was erected after a public campaign for such a memorial, was commissioned and supported by the Burma Plaque Appeal Committee, Bristol City Council, local businesses and various organisations. The inscription is surmounted by the badge of the Burma Star Association.

EMILY HARRIET SMITH JP (1860-1944)
PLAQUE: RICHMOND HOUSE, CLIFTON ROAD, BS8 1BS

Emily Harriet Smith was a pioneer of the women's suffrage movement and a trailblazer for the contribution she made to civic life in Bristol.

She was the first woman Unionist councillor in the city and the first woman to serve on the council's Watch, Libraries and Housing committees. She was also one of the first three women magistrates to sit on the Bristol Bench. Another of her interests was higher education and she became a member of the Court of Bristol University.

A plaque celebrating her life and work is on the front wall of Richmond House, a late eighteenth-century building in Clifton Road. Besides giving an outline of the bodies with which she was involved the inscription says that Emily Harriet Smith 'lived here from 1868–1944'.

ROBERT SOUTHEY (1774-1843)
POET LAUREATE, BIOGRAPHER, TRAVEL WRITER
PLAQUE: WINE STREET, BS1 2PH

Poet Laureate Robert Southey was born in Bristol, baptised and married in the city, yet today his name and his work is largely unknown here. He was born in Wine Street above his father's drapery business and his name appears in the baptismal registers of Christ Church, just a few yards around the corner from his birthplace.

He married Elizabeth Fricker in November 1795 at St Mary Redcliffe church. She was the sister of Sara Fricker, who had married the poet Samuel Taylor Coleridge at the same church just a month earlier. Southey was lent the money for his wedding licence and the ring by his publisher Joseph Cottle, who had a business on High Street Corner.

Although best known as a poet – he was appointed Poet Laureate in 1813 – Southey was a prolific writer of prose. His books include *A History of Brazil* and *A History of the Peninsular War*. He also produced biographies of prominent people including John Wesley, the founder of Methodism, and Oliver Cromwell, essays, ballads and travel books. Also to Southey's credit is a little tale called *The Three Bears* which became a children's classic and is the original Goldilocks story.

For a while Southey lived at Westbury-on-Trym before moving to Greta Hall, Keswick, in the Lake District, where he remained until his death forty years later.

Southey's birthplace has long disappeared to be replaced by a non-descript office block on which there is a stone plaque erected by the city council and surmounted by its coat of arms that says, 'In a house near this site was born Robert Southey'.

JESSIE STEPHEN (1893-1979)

SUFFRAGETTE AND POLITICAL PARTY ACTIVIST

PLAQUE: 27 CHESSEL STREET, BS3 3DP

Jessie Stephen dedicated most of her life to campaigning for women's votes and workers rights.

She was brought up in Glasgow, the eldest of eleven children, and won a scholarship to train as a teacher. However, her family's financial circumstances dictated otherwise and she became a domestic servant at the age of 15. A year later, Jessie was organising the Scottish Domestic Workers' Union and then helped to form the Scottish Federation of Domestic Workers. She also went to America and Canada to address meetings of English migrant domestic workers.

She moved to London to work in the suffrage movement — having been approached by Slyvia Pankhurst — and organised activities for the Women's Social and Political Union.

In Bristol Jessie became the first woman president of the city's Trades Council. She was also elected to the city council in 1952 as a Labour councillor for the Windmill Hill ward. She was also a candidate in parliamentary elections.

In 1955 Jessie was presented with the Trades Union Congress Gold Badge and in 1977 she was awarded an MBE; both honours were in recognition of her services to the trade union movement.

She died in Bristol General Hospital aged 86. Bristol City Council has fixed a blue plaque to the front of the house in Bedminster in which Jessie Stephen lived for many years until her death.

SIR ROBERT STEPHENS (1931–1995)

STAGE AND FILM ACTOR

PLAQUE: 34 PRIORY ROAD, BS11 9TD

From the back streets of the Bristol suburb of Shirehampton, where he was born, Robert Stephens rose to become one of the most respected actors of his generation. It was all the more remarkable as no one in his immediate family had ever trod the boards. His father was a shipyard worker and his mother worked at the Fry's chocolate factory in Bristol.

After a secondary education at the local Portway School — now the Oasis Academy Brightstowe — Robert won a two-year scholarship to Bradford Civic Theatre School in Yorkshire. It was there that he met the first of his four wives.

His theatrical career began on the provincial stage before he joined the newly established English Stage Company at the Royal Court in London in the 1950s. Robert made a name for himself as an actor in the title role of John Osborne's *Epitaph for George Dillon*.

Robert was invited to become one of the fifty founding members of Sir Laurence Olivier's National Theatre, later the Royal National Theatre. It was with this company that he met the actress Maggie Smith, later

Dame Maggie Smith, who became the third of his four wives. The couple were one of the most famous acting partnerships in British theatre, appearing together in many stage productions as well as films including *The Recruiting Officer* at the Old Vic and in the screen version of *The Prime of Miss Jean Brodie*. The couple married in 1967 but were divorced seven years later. They had two sons who both became actors.

Later in his career Robert became an acclaimed Shakespearean actor, appearing as Falstaff and taking the title role in *King Lear*. He appeared in plays and films for almost forty years and was knighted in 1995. Towards the end of that year he died in hospital due to complications during surgery after suffering poor health for some years. He was 64 years old.

A blue plaque celebrating his theatrical career and recording that he lived the first eight years of his life in Shirehampton was unveiled at his birthplace in Priory Road, Shirehampton, by the Lord Mayor.

THE RT REV. MERVYN STOCKWOOD (1913–1995)

CLERGYMAN

PLAQUE: CORNER OF CHURCH ROAD, COWPER STREET, BS5 9JZ

One of the Church of England's most senior bishops, the Right Reveverend Mervyn Stockwood, was given the nickname the 'Red Bishop' on account of his outspoken views.

Stockwood began his Church career in the impoverished Bristol parish of Moorfield, where he was ordained deacon in 1936 and priest the following year. Initially curate and then vicar of the parish, Stockwood served the parish for nineteen years. From inner-city Bristol he moved to Cambridge to be the vicar of Great St Mary, the university church. After only four years there he was offered the Bishopric of Southwark, a post he held for twenty years.

While he was in Bristol, Stockwood was elected to the city council as a Labour councillor for nine years.

It was while he was at Southwark that his liberal views on homosexuality, divorce, abortion and women priests earned him the sobriquet the 'Red Bishop'. Stockwood was one of the early advocates of women priests, a highly controversial issue in the Church of England. He went to America to ordain to the priesthood a woman whom he had previously ordained deacon in Southwark but at the time Church legislation barred her from the priesthood in England.

Stockwood's views were illustrated in his books *Christianity and Marxism* and *Cross and the Sickle*. While he was at Southwark the London diocese became one of the best known in the Church of England. He retired in 1980 and moved to Bath, where he died at the age of 82.

When a blue plaque honouring his contribution to Bristol was unveiled by the city's Lord Mayor it was said that 'the city was proud in honouring Mervyn Stockwood for his fearless pursuit of justice and determination in bringing about social reform'. The inscription on the plaque includes the tribute: 'As a Christian he inspired generosity. As a leader he fought for tolerance'. Fittingly, the plaque is fixed on what was St Matthew's church and is now flats on the corner of Cowper Street and Church Road.

RANDOLPH SUTTON (1888-1969)

SINGER AND ENTERTAINER

PLAQUE: 29 ANGLESEA PLACE, CLIFTON, BS8 2UN

Bristol-born Randolph Sutton gave up his job as a clerk to join a seaside concert party as a singer-cum-comedian. Audiences loved his humour and his home-spun songs with catchy titles like 'The Sun Has Got His Hat On', 'Mrs Rush and Her Scrubbing Brush' and 'My Canary Has Circles Under His Eyes'. Sutton is probably best remembered for his theme song 'On Mother Kelly's Doorstep' which was later adopted by the female impersonator Danny La Rue.

He went on tour around the country with his own show and became a popular music hall star who became known as Britain's premiere light comedian. Sutton made his first London appearance at the Pavilion in 1915, and thirty-three years later he took part in the Royal Variety Performance.

For many years Sutton was a radio and stage superstar. Audiences found it easy to sing along with his songs, which had become antidotes to the hard times of the depression of the 1930s and the war. As music hall went out of fashion, Sutton, being the professional trouper that he was, turned to making appearances in variety shows in theatres around the country. Sutton was also one of the first male principal boys in pantomime. His last appearance on stage was at the City Hall Theatre, St Albans on 28 February 1969. He died two days later aged 72.

Such was Sutton's popularity that after his death, Karl Denver, a Scottish singer, whose Western yodelling style was popular at the time, recorded 'My Canary Has Circles Under His Eyes' as a tribute. In another tribute the poet John Betjeman, a friend of Sutton's, made a television documentary about his showbusiness career.

The Clifton and Hotwells Improvement Society honoured Sutton by mounting one of their green plaques on the front of a cottage on the edge of Clifton and Durdham Downs where he was born. It was unveiled by a local actor, Chris Harris, who had played the role of Randolph Sutton in a television programme about the entertainer in 1969. The inscription on the plaque describes Sutton as a 'music hall star'.

JOHN ADDINGTON SYMONDS (1840-1893)

AUTHOR, POET AND LITERARY CRITIC

PLAQUES:
7 VICTORIA SQUARE, BS8 4EU
CLIFTON HILL HOUSE, LOWER CLIFTON HILL, BS8 1BX

John Addington Symonds, the son of an eminent Bristol doctor, had a prolific literary output, writing articles for leading periodicals, travel books, anthologies of poetry, studies of Dante and essays on the Greek poets. He was probably best known for his seven-volume *History of the Italian Renaissance*, which took him eleven years to complete. He also wrote biographies of Shelley, Sir Philip Sidney and Michelangelo.

Symonds was born in Berkeley Square, Clifton, and on his marriage to Catherine North in 1864, the couple settled in nearby Victoria Square. On his father's death Symonds inherited the Palladian Clifton Hill House, built on the slopes of Lower Clifton Hill, and lived there with his wife and four daughters. It was here that he wrote *An Introduction to the Study of Dante*.

Symonds was instrumental in founding University College, Bristol, in 1876 with many of the discussions leading up to its establishment taking place at his home.

Although he was married and was the father of four children, Symonds was an early advocate of homosexuality and openly referred to it in *The Meeting of David and Jonathan*, which he published in 1878. He publicly called for the subject to be discussed more openly and wanted the law against homosexuality relaxed.

Symonds is commemorated by two plaques in the city. One is outside his home in Victoria Square, which says that he 'lived here from 1865–71'. An engraved plaque on the wall of Clifton Hill House marks the time he lived there before his wedding and returning there from 1871–77 when he moved to Davos.

Poor health had forced Symonds to spend much of his time in Davos, Switzerland. As a sufferer of tuberculosis he found the climate in the world's highest city kinder to his health than in England. He died in Italy aged 53.

ROBERT TAYLOR (1920-1950)

BANK ROBBERY HERO

PLAQUE: 24 VICTORIA PARK. BS16 2HJ

Robert Taylor was posthumously awarded the George Cross for his selfless heroism as he tried to stop two armed bank robbers in their tracks. This award for gallantry takes precedence over all other orders, decorations and medals save for the Victoria Cross.

Mr Taylor, aged 29 at the time, who worked for the old *Bristol Evening World* newspaper, tried to rugby tackle the robbers as they escaped from Lloyds Bank, Westbury Park, in March 1950. He was shot in the face and unfortunately died in hospital.

Two Polish labourers, both in their early twenties, were arrested by the police in the nearby suburb of Redland, and put on trial. Both men pleaded not guilty to a charge of murder at Wiltshire Assizes. Mr Justice Oliver in his summing up of the trial told the jury: 'No argument in the world can dispose of the fact that a young man, doing nothing but his duty as a citizen, is by reason of doing so, shot down.' Both men were convicted of the charge and hanged at Winchester Prison.

Fifty-five years later, about thirty people – some of whom had known Robert Taylor and some from Lloyds Bank – gathered outside the house in Fishponds where he had lived all his life with his parents to witness the unveiling of a blue plaque praising Mr Taylor's bravery. This was the fortieth plaque that Bristol City Council had sponsored since it started asking the city's citizens to suggest the names of people that could be honoured.

HESTER THRALE (1741-1821)

FRIEND OF DR JOHNSON

PLAQUE: 20 SION HILL, BS8 4AZ

A commemorative green plaque on a house overlooking Clifton Suspension Bridge marks the life of Hester Thrale, an early eighteenth-century diarist and confidante of the writer and critic Dr Samuel Johnson.

After her husband Henry Thrale, a brewer from Southwark, London, died Mrs Thrale was expected to marry Dr Johnson. However, she surprised society by marrying Gabriel Piozzi, an Italian music teacher.

Her detailed diaries are an important source of information about Dr Johnson and provide a fascinating insight into daily life in Georgian society. After Dr Johnson died she published in 1786 *Anecdotes of Dr Johnson*. Two years later she published her letters.

The plaque, unveiled by Clifton and Hotwells Improvement Society, records that Hester Thrale was living on Sion Hill, Clifton, in 1821 when she died at the age of 80.

BEN TILLETT (1860-1943)

TRADE UNION LEADER AND POLITICIAN

PLAQUE: BANNERMAN ROAD, BS ORR

Ben Tillett is described on a memorial plaque as a 'tireless and determined defender of workers' rights'.

He led the London dockers' strike of 1889 when 130,000 men withdrew their labour. As general secretary of the Wharf, Riverside and General Workers Union he played a leading role during the early 1920s in the subsequent formation of the Transport and General Workers' Union. In 1918 he was elected a Member of Parliament and went on to become an alderman of London County Council and President of the Trades Union Congress in 1929.

Tillett was also one of the founders of the *Daily Herald* in 1912, a newspaper supporting the Labour movement. The paper was published for about fifty years until it folded in the early 1960s.

Tillett was born into poverty — the eighth and last child of his parents — in John Street, Easton.

His memorial plaque breaks away from the traditional oval or circular shape. It is a square bas-relief moulded plaque with a centrepiece portrait of Ben Tillett set against a docklands background. It was designed by local artist Mike Baker and is part of the Easton Time Signs Trail. The plaque is mounted on a wall in Bannerman Road, Easton, facing a small park, which was once John Street. It was unveiled in 2000 by Bill Morris, a former general secretary of the Transport and General Workers' Union, which had sponsored it.

DAME EVA TURNER (1892-1990)

INTERNATIONAL OPERA STAR

PLAQUE: BLOOMFIELD ROAD, BS4 3QT

Eva Turner was a Lancashire girl who moved to Bristol with her family when her father was appointed chief engineer of a cotton mill in the city.

She went to primary school in the St Anne's district, and was given singing lessons. In her early teens she was sent to the Royal Academy of Music, London. Her musical career took off when she joined the chorus of the Carl Rosa Opera Company after graduating from the Academy. A member of the management team, who was a specialist in voice training, coached Eva. This led to Eva taking on leading roles at the opera company's London season.

With a letter of recommendation Eva went to Italy in 1924 to audition for the renowned conductor Arturo Toscanini at La Scala. He hired her on the spot and she quickly became the leading dramatic soprano at La Scala in Milan. She took the title role in the first performance of Puccini's opera *Turandot* in 1926.

Several seasons at London's Covent Garden followed and during the Second World War Eva gave concerts for servicemen. Her international fame spread as she toured Europe to appear on stage in Austria, Spain and Portugal.

A plaque at St Anne's Primary School, Brislington, says that 'Eva Turner attended here from 1901–1906 and lived nearby'.

ADA VACHELL (1866-1923)

CHAMPION OF THE POOR

PLAQUES:
130 HAMPTON ROAD, BS6 6JE; BRISTOL CATHEDRAL, BS1 5TJ

Ada Vachell, who became known as Sister Ada, devoted much of her life to helping poor and disabled people. She set up social clubs which she said were for 'factory girls and crippled boys', and in 1895 founded the Guild of the Poor Things, although its name was later changed to the Guild of the Handicapped. Ada had the idea of getting disabled people together to combat boredom and isolation. By working with each other they could overcome their disabilities as far as possible and improve their lives.

Sister Ada went on to find apprenticeships for some of the young people and took as many guild members as she could on holiday each summer. It was not unknown for her to give baths each day to about twenty people staying in a farmhouse without a bathroom. In 1906 Sister Ada was able to buy a home at Churchill in Somerset for the guild. It became a purpose-built holiday centre. No longer was Sister Ada dependent on the kindness of country folk in providing accommodation.

Although she had a band of voluntary helpers Ada Vachell was always at the heart of the guild, dealing with everything from fund-raising to visiting disabled people in the workhouse.

She died suddenly of pneumonia at her home in Redland a few days after Christmas in 1923. Hundreds of people, many of whose lives had been touched by Ada's many acts of kindness, attended her funeral service at Bristol Cathedral.

A plaque in the cathedral commemorating Ada's work bears the emblem of the Guild of the Handicapped, a crutch and a sword. A blue plaque outside Ada Vachell's home in Hampton Road, Redland, describes her as 'Champion of poor and disabled people'. It records that she lived in the house from 1910 until her death.

PAULE VÉZELAY (1892-1984)

ABSTRACT ARTIST

PLAQUE: RODNEY PLACE. BS8 4HY

Clifton and Hotwells

PAULE VÉZELAY
(MARJORIE WATSON-WILLIAMS)
(1892-1984)

ABSTRACT ARTIST

LIVED HERE
1939-1942

Improvement Society

Marjorie Watson-Williams was the daughter of a distinguished Bristol ear, nose and throat surgeon who was also an amateur artist. She was educated at Clifton High School for Girls, not far from her home, and studied art initially in Bristol before enrolling at the London School of Art. Her work was put on show in London for the first time in 1921.

Five years later Marjorie moved to Paris where she produced her first abstract work. It was while she was in Paris that she changed her name to Paule Vézelay for professional purposes.

At the start of the Second World War she returned to Clifton to look after her parents. She drew scenes of some of the bomb damage caused during the Bristol Blitz of 1940–41.

After the war Paule Vézelay returned to London where she gained fame as one of the earliest abstract artists in Britain. Her works are included in many of the major art collections in Britain. She continued to work right up until her death at the age of 91.

Paule Vézelay is recognised for her talent by a plaque, erected by Clifton and Hotwells Improvement Society, outside a house in Rodney Place, Clifton. It records that the 'abstract artist lived here from 1939–1942'.

JOHN WALL (1855-1915)

SHOEMAKER AND POET

PLAQUE: CROYDON HOUSE. CROYDON STREET. BS5 0DX

John Wall was a cobbler who devoted much of his spare time to writing poetry. He sent an anthology of his verses to King Edward VII, whose secretary acknowledged receipt of the book and passed on the king's thanks.

Wall left school when he was 13 years old and was apprenticed to become a clicker in the boot and shoe trade with the Bristol and District Co-operative Society. As a clicker he cut the uppers or leather top part of boots and shoes. He eventually opened his own business, which he called the Shakespeare Boot Mart. He advertised that 'every part' of his business on Croydon Street, Easton Road, was under his 'direct oversight'.

A man with co-operative and socialist principles, Wall fought for the rights of working-class people. He was general secretary of the Boot Cutters Union and later secretary of Bristol Trades Council. Wall also organised free evening classes for working people.

Much of his literary work, which included writing poetry, novels, romances and short stories, focused on class inequality, unemployment and poverty. Wall drafted his poetry and novels on any scrap of paper that could be found, from the backs of posters and advertising leaflets to used envelopes. Bringing up six children on a low pay packet meant that there was no place in the family budget to buy proper writing paper.

A blue plaque recognising Wall's support for working-class people is fixed to Croydon House, a block of flats in Easton, located near the site of his shoe business, which has long been demolished to make way for redevelopment of the area.

FABIAN WARE (1869–1949)

FOUNDER COMMONWEALTH WAR GRAVES COMMISSION

PLAQUE: CLIFTON DOWN. BS8 3BP

The British Army rejected Fabian Ware as being too old for front-line service in the First World War. He was in his mid-forties. Instead of fighting the enemy on the Western Front he found himself in France commanding a mobile ambulance unit provided by the British Red Cross Society.

He was surprised that there wasn't any official system for recording the names of the war dead or marking their graves, so Fabian Ware set about establishing an organisation to do this. In 1915 both he and his organisation were transferred to the British Army and by May 1917 the Imperial (now Commonwealth) War Graves Commission was established by royal charter. The Prince of Wales was the Commission's president and Fabian Ware its vice chairman, a role he held until he retired in 1948.

Ware insisted that the headstones of all the graves of those killed in the war should be of the same design, with no distinction of rank, race or creed.

During his time in France Ware was twice mentioned in despatches and was ultimately promoted to the rank of major general. In the Second World War he was appointed director of Graves Registration and Enquiries at the War Office. At the same time he carried on his role at the War Graves Commission.

Ware was knighted in 1922. He died aged 80, a year after he retired, at his home in Gloucestershire. The director of the War Graves Commission unveiled a green plaque, donated by the Clifton and Hotwells Improvement Society, honouring Fabian Ware at his birthplace, Glendower House, Clifton Down in Bristol, in 2005.

JOHN (1703-1791) AND CHARLES WESLEY (1707-1788)

FOUNDER OF THE METHODIST CHURCH AND HYMN WRITER RESPECTIVELY

PLAQUE:　4 CHARLES STREET, ST JAMES BARTON, BS1 3NN

The brothers John and Charles Wesley and Methodism will forever be linked with Bristol. John has gone down in history for buying a plot of land in The Horsefair and building on it the world's first Methodist chapel, the New Room, which was opened in 1739. As well as being a place of worship, it had a schoolroom and a dispensary where the poor could get medicine. Today, Wesley's New Room finds itself sandwiched between large departmental stores, but it is still a mecca for thousands of pilgrims from all over the world each year.

John Wesley travelled some 25,000 miles around the country on horseback to preach at open-air meetings but he often returned to the New Room and lodged with his younger hymn-writing brother Charles, who lived nearby.

Charles is credited with writing some 6,500 hymns including the ever-popular 'Love Divine, All Love Excelling', 'Jesus Lover of My Soul' and the Christmas Carol, 'Hark The Herald Angels Sing'.

Some of his hymns were written in the five-storey eighteenth-century townhouse in St James Barton, not far from the New Room. A plaque outside No.4 Charles Street says that this was the home of Charles and his wife Sarah from 1749–71. It also says that it was here that their son, Samuel, was born. By the age of 5 Samuel could read music and three years later he had composed an oratorio called 'Ruth'. Samuel became a noted composer and organist and was considered to be a great exponent of the works of Bach.

SIR GEORGE WHITE (1854-1916)

AIRCRAFT PIONEER

PLAQUE:　ANCHOR ROAD, BS1 5LL

George White was born into relative poverty. His father was a painter and decorator, his mother a lady's maid. He left school at 14 and carved himself a glittering career which saw him setting up a new aeronautical industry in Britain which was based in Bristol.

His first job was as an office junior in a local firm of commercial lawyers. After just two years with the company he took charge of the bankruptcy side of the business and was said to be capable of looking after as many as a dozen liquidations at any one time. When he was 18 White formed the syndicate which became the Bristol Tramway and Carriage Company.

It wasn't long before he set himself up as a stockbroker and public accountant, specialising in transport shares. He bought into failing railway and tramway companies all over the country and made them profitable. The local press revelled in his financial deals, the type of which would normally be carried out by high-flying accountants and finance brokers in the City of London.

Although White is renowned for opening the first electric tramway service in the United Kingdom, in his home city he is best remembered for founding the British and Colonial Aeroplane Company (later the Bristol Aeroplane Company) in 1910 at Filton. The site has now become one of the largest aerospace complexes in Europe. Amongst the first aircraft that White's firm built were the Bristol Boxkite, the Scout, and the Bristol Fighter. By the outbreak of the First World War his flying schools had trained 308 of the 664 pilots available to fly. He also created a chain of 'aeroplane stations' (airports) across England.

In later life he became a philanthropist and was largely responsible for raising enough funds to build a major extension to the Bristol Royal Infirmary.

George White was made a baronet in 1904. He died suddenly in 1916. Despite the major contribution that he made to British industry it wasn't until 2014 that a plaque celebrating his life and work appeared in a prominent position in the centre of Bristol. It was erected on the engineers' wall of fame in Anchor Road, instituted by the Retired Professional Engineers' Club. This particular plaque was sponsored by Airbus.

RALPH VAUGHAN WILLIAMS (1872-1958)

COMPOSER

PLAQUE: SHIREHAMPTON PUBLIC HALL, STATION ROAD, BS11 9TX

The world premiere of 'The Lark Ascending' by the composer Ralph Vaughan Williams was staged in an unprepossessing public hall at Shirehampton, at the time a village on the north-west outskirts of Bristol.

This unusual venue was chosen as Vaughan Williams regularly visited a friend, Philip Napier Miles, who lived at nearby Kings Weston House. He was regarded as the village squire and prominent locally for his patronage of the arts, and conducting a choral society. Vaughan Williams started writing 'The Lark Ascending' in 1914 before the First World War but his musical activities came to a temporary halt when he joined the army.

The musician, considered by many people to be England's foremost symphonic composer, wrote 'The Lark Ascending' for violinist Miss Marie Hall, a protégé of Philip Miles. After the war ended Vaughan Williams and Miss Hall worked together at Kings Weston House to revise the piece of music to create a version for solo violin and piano. Its premiere was staged at Shirehampton Public Hall in 1920 in conjunction with Avonmouth and Shirehampton Choral Society. Today, 'The Lark Ascending' is often voted by music-lovers as their favourite piece of classical music.

In 2009 a brass plaque commemorating the premiere, fixed to the door of Shirehampton Public Hall, was unveiled by Em Marshall, the chairman of the Vaughan Williams Society. The event was followed by a performance of 'The Lark Ascending'.

CATHERINE (1827-1878) AND SUSANNA WINKWORTH (1820-1884)

HYMNOLOGISTS

PLAQUES:
31 CORNWALLIS CRESCENT, BS8 4PH
BRISTOL CATHEDRAL, BS1 5TJ

Every autumn, church congregations all over the country lustily sing hymns like 'Now Thank We All Our God', vainly trying to raise the roof at Harvest Festival services. The hymn is one of several hundred that were translated from the German into English.

This was done by Catherine Winkworth, who became fluent in the German language after living in Dresden for a year. She brought out the first series of her *Lyra Germanica*, with more than 100 congregational hymns for the Christian year, in about 1854. The hymns were so popular that twenty-three editions were published. She published a second series with more than 120 German hymns four years later and that ran into twelve editions. Many of the hymns that Catherine translated like 'Praise to the Lord the Almighty' and 'Christ the Lord is Risen Again' are still popular today.

Catherine and her sister Susanna, who were both born in London but brought up in Manchester, moved to Bristol in 1862. Both sisters became involved with local issues; Catherine championed the cause of higher education for women while Susanna pioneered what would be described today as social housing.

Catherine was a founder-governor of Clifton College and a governor of The Red Maids' School, now based at Westbury-on-Trym. Red Maids' proudly claims to be the oldest girls' school in the country, being founded in 1634. Catherine was also one of the promoters of Clifton High School for Girls, a member of the committee that helped establish University College, Bristol, the forerunner of the University of Bristol, and a member of the council of Cheltenham Ladies' College.

She died suddenly of heart disease at Monnetier in France while on a visit to Europe. In her memory Catherine's friends endowed two scholarships bearing her name at University College.

Meanwhile, Susanna was providing housing for poor people. In 1874 she formed the Bristol Industrial Dwelling Company, which was launched with £20,000 capital in £50 shares. Three blocks of tenements were built on Jacob's Wells Road.

Not only did Susanna help in designing the accommodation for eighty people but also managed the housing development until her death in 1884. Her tenement buildings survived until the 1950s when they were demolished, as they were considered to be substandard.

Catherine and Susanna Winkworth are remembered by a plaque, donated by the Clifton and Hotwells Improvement Society, marking the years they lived on Cornwallis Crescent, Clifton, from 1862–74. Another plaque, commemorating Catherine's translation of 'the treasurers of German sacred poetry' is on the east wall of Bristol Cathedral.

EMILY HILDA YOUNG (1880-1949)

AUTHOR

PLAQUE: 2 SAVILLE PLACE. BS8 4EJ

Although she used Bristol as a background for some of her novels, Emily Young is hardly, if ever, remembered in the city today. She disguised Clifton as Upper Radstowe in seven of her novels. Various streets like The Mall, for example, and Canynge Square took on new identities, becoming The Barton and Chatterton Square respectively. Emily also used Hotwells and the City Docks as settings. Bristol had obviously made a deep impression on her for many of her novels were written between 1922 and 1947, some years after she had left the city.

Writing under the name E.H. Young she published a number of novels, several of which were adapted for broadcast as radio plays. There are also short stories and children's books to her credit. Her Bristol-based novels were re-published in the 1980s.

She arrived in Bristol from Northumberland and married Arthur Daniell, a local solicitor. They settled into a top-floor flat in Saville Place, off Regent Street, Clifton. During the First World War Emily worked as a stable groom and later in a munitions factory, probably the one the government set up at Avonmouth, 7 miles from her home.

Emily Young's romantic life could well have been the stuff of a novel itself. After her husband died during the First World War in a battle in Ypres, she headed to London and lived in a *ménage à trois* with Ralph Henderson, who had been a friend of her husband's; Henderson's wife was living in the same house. When Henderson retired from the headship of Alleyne's School, Dulwich, he and Emily moved to Bradford-on-Avon, Wiltshire, where she lived for the rest of her life.

A green plaque marking the years that Emily Young lived in Saville Place from 1907–1918 has been mounted on the facade of the house by Clifton and Hotwells Improvement Society.

PROFESSOR JOHN ZIMAN (1925-2005)

THEORETICAL SCIENTIST

PLAQUE: EASTFIELD LODGE. BS9 4AD

A goodly crowd of councillors, university representatives, dozens of pupils from the nearby Red Maids' School and relatives of Professor John Ziman turned up for the ceremony when the first blue plaque was unveiled in the Westbury-on-Trym neighbourhood by the Lord Mayor in 2008.

The plaque commemorates Professor Ziman, who for eighteen years from 1964 held the professorial chair of theoretical physics at Bristol University.

Three years after his arrival at the university he was elected to the Royal Society and shortly after that he published his first philosophical book *Public Knowledge*. A stream of papers and books followed.

Professor Ziman left Bristol University in 1982 to take up a visiting professorship at Imperial College, London.

The inscription on the plaque which is fixed to the boundary wall of Eastfield Lodge, where Professor Ziman lived, describes him as a 'physicist, philosopher and humanist who explored the meaning of science in society'.

2

PLAQUES OF HISTORY

THE ROYAL FORT
PLAQUE: ROYAL FORT, TYNDALL'S ROAD, BS8 1TH

During the Civil War Bristol was besieged by both sides. Prince Rupert took it from Parliament in 1643, but two years later, after a month-long siege, he capitulated to General Fairfax and Oliver Cromwell.

Nearly four centuries on Bristol still has a most unusual reminder of the Civil War. The remains of a brick gatehouse are almost hidden amongst the twentieth-century buildings that make up Bristol University's campus.

ROYAL FORT-PRINCE RUPERT'S GATE

Near this spot, on 11 September 1645, Prince Rupert of the Rhine, nephew of King Charles I and Commander of the Royalist garrison of Bristol, surrendered the City to Sir Thomas Fairfax, Commander of Parliament's New Model Army and to Oliver Cromwell, his Master of Horse.

This brick gatehouse is the most substantial remaining portion of the Royal Fort, a pentagonal bastion reconstructed by Prince Rupert after he had captured Bristol in 1643.

Because of Bristol's strategic military position and value as a port, its capture by the Parliamentarian forces was a turning point of the Civil War.

Erected jointly by the Clifton and Hotwells Improvement Society and the University of Bristol

The remains of the Royal Fort gatehouse.

A plaque nearby tells us that this is the most substantial remaining portion of the Royal Fort, a pentagonal bastion reconstructed by Prince Rupert after he had captured the city in 1643.

Part of the inscription says that 'near this spot on 11 September 1645 Prince Rupert of Rhine, nephew of King Charles I and Commander of the Royal Garrison of Bristol, surrendered the city to Sir Thomas Fairfax, Commander of Parliament's new Model Army, and to Oliver Cromwell, his Master of Horse'.

Because of Bristol's strategic military position and value as a port, its capture by parliamentarian forces was a strategic turning point of the Civil War.

The large rectangular plaque at the Royal Fort was jointly installed by the Clifton and Hotwells Improvement Society and the University of Bristol.

WASHINGTON'S BREACH PLAQUE
QUEEN'S ROAD, BS8 1RL

A bronze plaque outside Bristol Museum on Queens Road, Clifton, honours Colonel Henry Washington, an ancestor of the former American president. This Royalist colonel confounded the parliamentary troops holding Bristol in the Civil War by breaching their defences. He did it by arming his force of dragoons with 'fire pikes'. Apparently, the blazing pikes unnerved the Roundhead troopers that they deserted the ramparts and let through the attacking Royalists.

The inscription on the plaque states: 'From near this spot on 26 July 1645 Colonel Henry Washington attacked the parliamentary defence between Royal Fort and Brandon Hill. With a small force he affected "Washington's Breach" at the present junction of Park Street and Park Row through which the Royalist troops entered Bristol and compelled its capitulation'.

Colonel Washington was the grandson of Lawrence Washington of Sulgrave and a collateral ancestor of George Washington, the first President of the United States of America. The plaque was erected by the Bristol branch of the Geographical Association.

CROMWELL'S COUNCIL OF WAR
PLAQUE: PARK ROAD. BS16 1DG

Two key figures on the parliamentarian side in the Civil War held a Council of War at a house in Stapleton before an attack on Bristol in 1645.

Oliver Cromwell and his right-hand man General Sir Thomas Fairfax held their meeting at Wickham Court, now a Grade II Listed building. Hours later a raid was launched on Bristol by the parliamentarians. The signal that this was about to start was given by the sound of cannon shot booming out across the city at 2 a.m. on 10 September 1645.

It led to weeks of bloody fighting with hundreds of people losing their lives. The raid ended one of the longest sieges in the Civil War.

The Royalist commander Prince Rupert was eventually forced to surrender the city that he had taken from the parliamentarians in 1643 to General Fairfax, Commander of the parliamentary New Model Army.

The Council of War is recalled in an oblong blue plaque with just six lines of text mounted on a side wall of the six-bedroom Wickham Court. This seventeenth-century Grade II Listed building stands in a cul-de-sac at Park Road, Stapleton.

3

AMERICAN CONNECTIONS

THE AMERICAN EMBASSY
PLAQUE: 37 QUEEN SQUARE, BS1 4QS

Tree-lined Queen Square, with all its Georgian elegance, is said to be the largest perfect square in England with all its sides being equal. It was originally laid out at the start of the eighteenth century. The square can also lay claim to being the location of the first American consulate in Great Britain. It was set up in a house on the southern side of the square close to the docks in September 1792. This was just three years after George Washington had been made the first president of the United States of America.

Bristol may have been chosen for the consulate because of its long history of exploration to the New World, as well as its trade with America.

The first consul was Elias Vanderhorst, a native of South Carolina, who had been living with his family in Bristol for the previous eighteen years. As consul his duties included caring for fellow Americans living in Bristol. A plaque on No.37 Queen Square, a Grade II* Listed building, says that the consulate was founded 'in a house on this site'.

BITS OF BRISTOL IN AMERICA
PLAQUE: THE QUAY HEAD, BS1

One of a trail of plaques at The Quay Head – most of them with a nautical theme – is a replica of one on East River Drive, Bristol Basin in New York. It marks the location of where some of the stones, bricks and rubble from the bombing of Bristol, England, during the Second World War arrived in the United States of America as ballast in boats.

Some 3,000 properties in Bristol, from churches and homes to offices to shops and factories, were destroyed during the war and nearly 100,000 properties damaged. This was mainly during the blitz on the city in 1940–41. The ruins of some of the bombed buildings went to America in empty ships that had brought much-need supplies to Britain. The debris was used as a foundation to build East River Drive.

In 1942 a plaque commemorating this unusual link between Bristol and America was unveiled at a special ceremony attended by marines from Britain and the Mayor of New York. The wording of the plaque headed Bristol Basin says, 'These fragments that once were homes shall testify while men love freedom to the resolution and fortitude of the people of Britain. They saw their homes struck down without warning'.

The inscription reminds a new generation of the debt that all who hold freedom dear owe to those in Britain, especially those in Bristol who lost so much in its name.

By the time work had started on redeveloping Bristol Basin in 1970 the plaque had disappeared. However, the English Speaking Union stepped in when the redevelopment scheme was finished four years later and organised a ceremony for a replacement plaque to be unveiled. It was dedicated by the Bristol-born Hollywood film star Cary Grant.

4

TRANSPORT
AND TRAVEL

SS GREAT WESTERN
PLAQUE: QUAYSIDE SHEDS, WAPPING WHARF, BS1 4RN

While working as engineer to the Great Western Railway, Isambard Kingdom Brunel conceived the idea of building steamships for the Bristol to New York route.

He designed the SS *Great Western*, which was the largest passenger ship in the world at the time. The ship cost £65,000 and was launched in 1837. The *Great Western* worked the Atlantic route for eight years until her owners went out of business. She was then sold to the Royal Mail Steam Packet Company and later served as a troopship during the Crimean War. She was eventually scrapped in 1856.

A plaque on the side of an old dockside shed states that the ship was launched 'near this spot' on 19 July 1837. It also records that the 230ft-long ship made its first voyage from Bristol to New York in April 1838. But strangely there's no mention that the ship was designed by Isambard Kingdom Brunel.

ROYAL WESTERN HOTEL

(NOW KNOWN AS BRUNEL HOUSE)

PLAQUE: CORNER OF ST GEORGE'S ROAD/BRANDON STEEP, BS1 5UY

It wasn't just railways, bridges and ships with which the engineer Isambard Kingdom Brunel was involved. He also worked with the local architect Richard Shackleton Pope to create a hotel with a classical facade.

Brunel wanted the Royal Western Hotel to accommodate passengers travelling to and from America on his steamship the *Great Western*, which was built in Bristol. Passengers would board the train at Paddington heading for Bristol on Brunel's Great Western Railway and then transfer to his elegant hotel before embarking on the steamship the next day. Brunel's scheme was seen as an early form of integrated transport system.

The hotel was opened in 1838 amidst much pomp and ceremony with the Lord Mayor of Bristol being guest of honour at an inaugural banquet. Unfortunately, the city's bid for the transatlantic trade was a flop. The *Great Western* was forced by the Cunard shipping line to make Liverpool her port of call and not Avonmouth. It meant that just a few years after it opened Brunel's hotel had closed and was turned by another entrepreneur into a Turkish bath.

Brunel House, formerly the Royal Western Hotel.

The hotel building still stands although it was threatened with demolition in the 1960s, despite the old Ministry of Housing describing it as 'one of the finest monumental buildings in the West of England'. It was placed on the government's Grade II list of buildings of architectural merit and given a facelift whilst its splendid facade with ionic columns was kept. The building, now known as Brunel House, is used as overspill offices for council staff from City Hall on the opposite side of the road.

In what appears to be just a nod to the building's history, a very small plaque recording its original use is fixed to one of its side walls. It's in such an inconspicuous position that the thousands of office workers and shoppers who pass Brunel House in St George's Road each day are totally unaware of its back story.

CUMBERLAND BASIN FLYOVER
PLAQUE: BRUNEL LOCK ROAD, BS1 6XS

So many councillors, council officials and contractors were involved with the construction of the Cumberland Basin flyover scheme that three large bronze plaques were needed so that all their names could be recorded for public posterity.

Taking pride of place is the name of Tom Fraser MP, Minister of Transport, who officially opened the flyover in April 1965. His name is followed by that of the Lord Mayor of Bristol, who heads what seems to be a catalogue of aldermen and councillors. Not to be forgotten is the all-important city engineer, assistant engineer, resident engineers and principal assistant engineer. The third plaque bears the names of the contractors, surveyors and landscape architects.

The plaques are fixed to a rather grand concrete memorial on a promontory of the banks of the River Avon below the Cumberland Basin flyover. It stands where few people ever wander.

The Cumberland Basin flyover spanning the River Avon comprises a bridge at the entrance lock, the Plimsoll swing bridge over the River Avon, and interchanges which link up with nearby roads. The scheme cost £2.5 million and took two years to build. An inscription on one of the plaques says this was the first project of its kind to be built in Bristol.

Three plaques on a plinth below the Cumberland Basin flyover.

It was designed to assist traffic flow by the use of roads at different levels, especially when the Plimsoll Bridge swings open to let ships in and out of the City Docks. Roads, homes, shops and pubs at Hotwells close to the site were bulldozed to make way for the flyover.

BOYCOTT ON THE BUSES
PLAQUE: MARLBOROUGH STREET. BS1 3NU

For the many thousands of travellers who use Bristol bus station each day the story behind a three-dimensional plaque depicting four West Indian men must come as something of a shock. It tells of an episode in the city's history which would be unimaginable today.

The four men were at the forefront of a campaign to boycott the buses because Bristol Omnibus Company refused to employ non-white people as conductors or drivers, despite the presence of an established Caribbean community in the city. Four months to the day after the boycott was announced the bus company said it would lift its ban.

Organisers of the boycott in 1963 believe it played a major part in getting Parliament to pass the Race Relations Act in 1965. This made 'racial discrimination unlawful in a public place'.

The struggle against racism in Bristol is recalled in the bas-relief moulded plaque at the city's bus station in Marlborough Street. Designed by local artist Mike Baker, the multi-coloured plaque not only depicts the leaders of the boycott, but also shows the bus company's headquarters, then in the city centre, against the background of a bus, a protest march and a West Indian man boarding a bus. A brief text explains the background to the boycott.

The plaque was organised by the Bristol Bus Group 50, a group of organisations and individuals formed to mark the fiftieth anniversary of the bus boycott. It was unveiled in 2014 by the Lord Mayor of Bristol at a ceremony attended by some of the leaders of the boycott.

5

PUBLIC HOUSES

LLANDOGER TROW
PLAQUE: KING STREET, BS1 4ER

This public house stands on a street sometimes known as Museum Street, on account of the architectural styles of its buildings which spans more than three centuries. One of the buildings is the Llandoger Trow, which dates back to the seventeenth century. It is also one of the last timber-framed buildings to be erected in Bristol; the Great Fire of London, which happened two years after the Llandoger Trow was built, put an end to this style of construction.

In its early years the pub only occupied one of the five original gables, the other four being occupied by businesses as diverse as a grocer's, a basket maker's and a tobacconist's. The exact time when the pub extended its size is unclear.

Tradition has it that it was in the Llandoger Trow that the writer Daniel Defoe met Alexander Selkirk, a sailor who had been marooned on the island of Juan Fernandez in the South Pacific Ocean for four years. He was rescued by the privateer Captain Woodes Rogers who lived in Queen Square near the pub and brought him to Bristol. Selkirk is said to have been the inspiration for Defoe's novel *Robinson Crusoe*, but there has never been any evidence that the two men met in this particular tavern.

An oval stone plaque, bearing the legend 'City and County of Bristol', on the side of the pub gives its date of construction as 1664. This makes it one of the oldest hostelries in the city. The inscription also tells us that the pub takes its name from the trows that came to the Welsh Back. Trows were flat-bottomed barges that traded between the Welsh village of Llandogo on the River Wye and the part of Bristol's Floating Harbour known as Welsh Back, close to the Llandoger pub.

THE BUSH TAVERN AND LLOYDS BANK
PLAQUE: CORN STREET, BS1 1HT

One of the works of Charles Dickens and the world of high finance come together on the same bronze plaque in what is now called Bristol's 'Old Quarter'. It is mounted on the wall of the bank building, which replaced the Bush Tavern in Corn Street. The plaque tells us that 'on this site stood the Bush Coaching Inn which was used by Edmund Burke' as his election campaign headquarters in 1774. It was here that he addressed crowds of supporters before he was elected to Parliament where he represented Bristol for six years.

It was also at the Bush that Dickens had Mr Winkle take up his quarters in his lovelorn quest for the missing Arabella Allen in his novel *The Pickwick Papers*.

The Bush Tavern had a reputation under one of its landlords, John Weeks, for serving up lavish banquets. He advertised his turtles – they were said to weigh anything from 40 to 200lbs – as being 'dressed daily'. Weeks also made the Bush Tavern one of the city's principal coaching inns. In 1775 he started running a stagecoach between Bristol and London in an unprecedented time of sixteen hours. Soon after that he started operating coaches to Oxford, Exeter and Birmingham. When rival operators threatened to run him off the road he gave his passengers a free dinner with wine in a bid to boost his trade.

The Bush Tavern was bought by the West of England and South Wales Bank for £10,000 and demolished in the late 1850s to make way for its headquarters. The architects based their High Renaissance style of the new building on Jacopo Sansovino's Library of St Mark's, Venice.

John Thomas, the artist responsible for overseeing the carvings on the Houses of Parliament, was asked to create the friezes that adorn this Grade II listed building. The frieze on the first floor has works depicting the 'elements and sources of wealth' which include justice and integrity, education and charity, peace and plenty, art and science, commerce and navigation. A frieze along the top of the building has carved cherubs depicting activities of the bank including receiving, paying, storing, coining, and printing money.

The West of England Bank crashed in 1878. Against its liabilities of about £350,000 there was a further deficiency of assets exceeding £300,000. Another finance house, this time Lloyds Bank, took over the building, which it occupied until January 2014 when it moved to new premises in the nearby Cabot Circus shopping and leisure centre. The plaque on the front of the building says that the exterior remains substantial in its original form.

THE HATCHET
PLAQUE: FROGMORE STREET. BS1 5NA

In Regency days The Hatchet pub was known not only for its ale but also the bare-knuckle boxing fights that took place in a ring set up at the back of the inn. Remarkably, five of the English bare-knuckle champions – Jem Belcher, Henry Pearce, Tom Cribb, John Gully and Ben Brain – came from Bristol or the surrounding area.

Perhaps the best-known was Tom Cribb, who was nicknamed 'The Black Diamond', a reference to his work in the coal trade. Cribb was only defeated once in thirty major fights. The record books show that this single defeat was at the hands of George Nicholls in 1805 and that was in the fifty-second round. When Cribb defeated the American boxer Tom Molineaux, the centre of London was brought to a standstill by the huge number of Cribb's followers who wanted to pay tribute to the champion. He held the title for ten years.

Cribb regularly fought at pubs in Bristol including The Hatchet, which dates back to 1606 and is one of the oldest pubs in the city. After retiring from the boxing ring Cribb went on to run a pub in London.

For two centuries the 'Bristol Boys' as they were known were generally ignored or forgotten. This all changed in 2011 when a book was written about them and a 3-dimensional plaque showing all five champions was unveiled on an outside wall of The Hatchet. The plaque, cast in aluminium and painted in enamel, was designed by local artist Mike Baker. On it he finds space to list the achievements of the five champions with portraits of each of them. Tom Cribb is given prominence in the centre of the plaque, depicted in action in a boxing ring with The Hatchet pub in the background. The plaque was unveiled by former boxing champion Glenn Catley.

THE STAG AND HOUNDS AND PIE POUDRE COURT
PLAQUE: OLD MARKET STREET, BS2 0EJ

A small wooden sign on the front of the Stag and Hounds pub in Old Market Street recalls the days when instant justice was dispensed to miscreants.

From the twelfth century onwards, Old Market Street was the site of a large market and fair, which served the nearby Bristol Castle. It attracted many hundreds of merchants, pedlars, and more than its fair share of rogues.

In Norman times a special court was set up to deal swiftly with the thieves and debtors who plagued the market. Known as Pie Poudre Court, it was held in the open air under an ancient oak tree, now the site of the Stag and Hounds pub. When the pub was built the court moved inside sitting in a large panelled upstairs room above the portico.

Pie Poudre Court was specifically intended for settling the many disputes that arose at the market. Its name is believed to have come from the old French: loosely translated it means 'dusty foot'. This is a reference to the swiftness with which justice was handed down – before defendants had time to shake the dust off their feet and escape judgement.

The only evidence of Pie Poudre Court is the plaque outside which simply states that 'the ancient court of the Pie Poudre was annually proclaimed from this portico'.

6

THE ENTERTAINMENT INDUSTRY

HIS MASTER'S VOICE (1884-1895)
PLAQUE: CORNER OF PARK ROW AND WOODLAND ROAD, BS1 5LT

High up on the wall of an office building on the corner of Park Row and Woodland Road is a statue of a dog carved in stone. Next to it is a blue plaque bearing the heading 'His Master's Voice'. Both are tributes to Nipper, a Jack Russell terrier who became an international trademark. He is probably the only canine in the country to be honoured in such a way.

Nipper was born in Bristol in 1884 and was so named because of his tendency to nip the backs of people's legs. His owner was Mark Baraud, a scenic designer at the Princes Theatre in Park Row, which opened in 1867.

When Mark died in 1887 his younger brother, Francis, gave Nipper a home and painted him listening to the family's horn gramophone. He sold the painting to a gramophone company for £100. The firm substituted their own gramophone and added the words 'His Master's Voice' to the painting.

It became a trademark with Nipper's image appearing on the labels of HMV (His Master's Voice) records, which were not only sold in this country but also overseas. Nipper also appeared in advertisements and on promotional items such as souvenir paperweights and ashtrays.

The plaque celebrating Nipper is on the wall of a building which stands on the site of the Princes Theatre opened in October 1867 and which was destroyed in the Blitz of Bristol of November 1940.

When Nipper died, after being a faithful friend to his two masters for a total of twenty-one years, he was laid to rest by Francis Baraud in the garden of his home in Surrey.

THE GAIETY CINEMA
PLAQUE: WELLS ROAD, KNOWLE, BS4 2SQ

At one time there was at least one cinema, if not two, in almost every suburb of Bristol. However, most picture houses, as they were popularly known, have disappeared without any trace whatsoever. They have been replaced by homes, car showrooms, pubs, supermarkets and a library. The Gaiety Cinema at Knowle was one of those that fell into the mouth of the bulldozers. However, unlike the others it will be remembered for some time to come thanks to a plaque on the exterior wall of the sheltered accommodation that now stands on its site.

The Gaiety Cinema was privately built by Roy Chamberlain, who also owned the nearby Knowle Picture House. He opened it on Boxing Day 1933 with a new film called *The Good Companions*, which starred Jessie Matthews and John Gielgud.

A local paper described the Gaiety as 'a new super cinema for a growing suburb'. The paper reported that the cinema had seating for 800 people and on the balcony level Mr Chamberlain had built a dance hall with a capacity for 125 people.

The Gaiety remained in the ownership of his family until 1991 when it was sold to Hallmark Cinemas. The following year the new owners converted the dance hall into a second cinema with seats for seventy-five people, and the year after that they installed a third screen in another part of the building. Despite these additions at the Gaiety its audiences were still dwindling. Filmgoers were being attracted to the new out-of-town cinema complexes. And not far from Knowle, a fourteen-screen cinema with a fast-food outlet and large car park on the site had opened at Avon Meads as part of an inner-city regeneration scheme.

All this led to the Gaiety's projectors being switched on for the final time in 1995, with screenings of *Pulp Fiction* and *Four Weddings and a Funeral* attracting fewer than a dozen film fans.

Inscribed on a blue plaque outside the sheltered accommodation are the words: 'On this site stood the Gaiety Cinema, the last family-owned cinema in Bristol which showed films to an estimated eight million people.'

7

INDUSTRY PLAQUES

GREAT WESTERN COTTON FACTORY
PLAQUE: MAZE STREET. BS5 9TE

We tend to think of cotton mills as being a significant part of the northern industrial scene but for the best part of a century Bristol had its own mill.

The Great Western Cotton Factory, designed by Isambard Kingdom Brunel, even had an international reputation, with its Barton Hill calico being exported to Gibraltar, Italy, India and China.

The mill was built on a 7-acre site at Barton Hill alongside the Feeder Canal and was close to the main railway lines, ideal for transporting the finished product. There were a number of buildings on the site including a spinning mill, which at six-stories high towered over Barton Hill, weaving sheds and outbuildings. Nearly 100,000 spindles and 1,600 looms were working almost full time.

The Great Western Cotton Factory opened in 1838 and at one time around 1,000 people were employed there. Many of them were girls aged 13 and 14. The last piece of cotton was spun in 1925, when the mill closed.

Three years later the factory re-opened under new ownership with the staff making artificial silk. This was a short-lived venture with the factory closing for a second time in the early 1930s. From then until 1968, when most of the buildings were demolished, they were put to various uses. At different times gun turrets were manufactured there and drums of milk powder, animal feed, and groceries were stored on the site waiting to be delivered to stores across Bristol.

The Barton Hill History Group and the Sovereign Housing Association, which has been involved in the regeneration of the area, commissioned a plaque in 2015 to remember those who toiled on poor pay in the harsh working conditions of the cotton mill. The bas-relief moulded plaque depicts the mill buildings with the inscription quoting Florence Weekes, one of the many women who worked at the factory in 1918, saying: 'Wages were low. I earned 15 shillings a week for 60 hours hard labour.'

This is another plaque designed by local artist and historian Mike Baker and cast by Wards of Bristol. It has been mounted on the outside of the firm's factory at Barton Hill, which is one of the last remaining buildings of the cotton factory.

J.S. FRY & SONS

CHOCOLATE MAKER

PLAQUE: UNION STREET, BS1

Joseph Fry was making his own chocolate, initially as a drink, in 1756. The family firm of J.S. Fry & Sons has the distinction of making the first commercial block of chocolate in the world at its factory in Bristol.

The demand for chocolate became so great that Fry's built seven factory blocks in the city and by the start of the twentieth century the company employed 4,600 people, mostly women, who were known as 'Fry's Angels'. All staff were expected to attend a service at the start of the day and hymn singing was encouraged during the working shift of twelve hours.

Fry's merged with rival chocolate maker Cadbury in 1919 but still traded under its family name. It later moved out of its factories in the Union Street area of Bristol to the Cadbury plant at Somerdale, Keynsham, 7 miles away from the smoke and grime of the city centre.

The only reminder of Fry's presence in the city is a plaque high up on wall in Union Street, now part of the Broadmead shopping centre. The text says: 'Near this site for over 200 years J.S. Fry & Sons manufactured cocoa and chocolate before moving to Somerdale in 1986'. In 2009 Cadbury's announced the closure of its Somerdale plant, saying that it was transferring some production to Poland.

EASTON COLLIERY
PLAQUE: FELIX ROAD. BS5 0JW

More than 3,000 men were working in the city's collieries at the start of the twentieth century. One of the collieries was at Easton and was in production for nearly a hundred years.

Explosions at collieries were, unfortunately, not uncommon. In February 1886 an explosion at Easton colliery claimed the lives of eight miners. One of the first people on the scene to administer first aid to the injured men was Dr W.G. Grace, the 'cricketing doctor', whose surgery was nearby.

The owners of the colliery abandoned mining in 1911 and put the 3-acre site, which included offices, under the auctioneer's hammer. For a while the site was used as a stone yard by a local firm of builders. Today the site, just over a mile from the city centre, is occupied by two business centres and Felix Road Adventure playground for children and young people.

A three-dimensional plaque, part of the Living Easton Time Signs Trail, was erected on the site on the twenty-fifth anniversary of the playground opening in 1997. It features scenes of both the playground and the colliery, helping to keep alive the memory of the coal trade.

BRISTOL CURIOSITIES

BRISTOL SYNAGOGUE CENTENARY
PLAQUE: PARK ROW, BS1 5LP

When the Bristol Hebrew Congregation celebrated the centenary of its synagogue at Park Row in 1971 it didn't have to look far for someone special to unveil a plaque marking this important milestone.

As the inscription on the plaque succinctly says: 'This plaque was unveiled ... by the Rt Hon. Lord Mayor of Bristol, Alderman Mrs Helen Bloom, the first Jewish Lord Mayor of Bristol.'

Alderman Bloom was only the third woman to hold the office of Lord Mayor in Bristol's history when she was appointed in 1971, although the city has had mayors, later Lord Mayors, since 1216.

The Park Row synagogue replaced one that stood near Temple Street but had to make way for a road-widening scheme.

BRISTOL TIME
PLAQUE: 40 COLLEGE GREEN, BS1 5SU

Measuring just over 2in in width and 1in in depth this must qualify as the smallest plaque in Bristol. Thousands of people walk over it each day but probably few realise they are doing so, for this plaque on College Green is embedded in the pavement.

Engraved on it is the legend that the correct solar time in Bristol is ten minutes and twenty-three seconds behind that calculated by the Royal Observatory at Greenwich – Greenwich Mean Time (GMT).

Although we now take GMT for granted, in the early Victorian period every city and town had its own local time, reckoned by the sun and signed by church bells. This was not a problem until the growth of the railways, running to GMT, so in 1852 Bristol adopted GMT, which has become the UK's standard time.

The plaque also records that in 1852 local watch and clockmaker William Langford took the time by telegraph wire from the Greenwich Royal Observatory. Langford worked in Bristol for nearly fifty years from 1828 and at one time his business premises were on College Green, at the site of the present plaque. It is sited under a Langford clock that took the time from Greenwich and still remains in place.

BRISTOL DOCKS ANNIVERSARY
PLAQUE: QUAY HEAD, BS1 5TX

Bristol Corporation, as the city council was known at the time, marked the 100th anniversary of civic ownership of the Bristol Docks on 30 June 1948 in some style. The corporation had bought the docks from the Bristol Dock Company, which had never achieved commercial success.

The celebrations included the unveiling of a large bronze plaque at the Quay Head close to the City Docks. It forms part of a trail of plaques charting important episodes in Bristol's history. Its inscription tells us that the plaque was unveiled by alderman A.W.S. Burgess JP, chairman of the port authority. This short ceremony was 'witnessed by the Lord Mayor, some of the city's Members of Parliament, councillors and many users of the port'.

Afterwards the guests embarked on the *Bristol Queen* paddle steamer for Avonmouth Docks, about 7 miles downstream, where luncheon was served.

Later, the council bought the slipway at Nova Scotia yard to enlarge the maintenance facilities for the docks.

BRISTOL ROYAL SCHOOL AND WORKSHOPS FOR THE BLIND
PLAQUE: HENLEAZE ROAD, BS9 4NL

The Bristol Royal School and Workshops for the Blind is the oldest institution of its kind in the world. It was instituted in 1793 and incorporated in 1832. In its early days the school stood on a site near Bristol University's Wills Memorial Building in Queens Road, Clifton.

In the early years of the twentieth century the school's buildings were sold to the university and the money for it was used for a new development on an 11-acre site in Henleaze. A new school for the blind opened in 1911 with the number of pupils, both boarders and day pupils, growing to 126 in the post Second World War years; they came from all over the country.

There were separate workshops in the grounds where older pupils could be trained in such things as basket making, machine knitting and the tuning of pianos.

However, the number of students in the 1960s had dwindled which brought about the school's closure. Along with its grounds it was sold to a developer who demolished the buildings and replaced them with an estate of ninety mock Georgian homes.

Former pupils of the school who believed there should be some kind of memorial on the estate recalling its history clubbed together to sponsor the erection of a blue plaque. In 2008 the Lord Mayor was assisted by a former pupil in unveiling the plaque which is in a prominent position on the housing estate's boundary wall at the end of Henleaze Road.

A ROYAL EVENT
PLAQUE: CLIFTON DOWN, BS8 3NB

The great and good of Bristol turned out in force for the planting of a tree opposite the Lord Mayor's Mansion House on Clifton Down, near the top of Bridge Valley Road. This was no ordinary tree-planting ceremony for it marked the coronation of a king.

The occasion also merited a plaque firmly embedded in the earth at the foot of this now mighty oak tree. Its inscription states that it was planted on the 'fourteenth day of March 1903 by the Lord Mayor'. The text goes on to say that this was done in 'the presence of the Lord Bishop of Bristol, the Master of the Society of Merchant Venturers and other citizens'.

The tree commemorates the coronation of 'His Majesty King Edward the Seventh' which had taken place seven months earlier in August 1902.

THE SLAVE TRADE
PLAQUE: M SHED. WAPPING WHARF. BS1 4RN

Historically, Bristol prospered through the three vices of wine, tobacco and slavery. As far as the latter was concerned the city was one of the main UK ports involved in the trading of slaves taken from West Africa to British colonies in the Caribbean.

Between 1697 and 1807, 2,108 known ships left Bristol to make the journey to Africa and onwards across the Atlantic Ocean with slaves. It has been estimated that some 3.4 million slaves were carried on those ships in appalling conditions. The bodies of those who died on the journey were thrown overboard into the sea.

Mention the slave trade today and passions become heated. There are those who believe that Bristol should officially apologise for its role in the trade and others who adopt an attitude of let's forget it, after all it happened 300 years ago and was a legal activity at the time.

The slave trade, now viewed with much abhorrence, is recalled in a plaque on the dockside. The inscription in raised white lettering on a black background begins: 'In memory of countless Africans, men, women and children whose enslavement and exploitation brought so much prosperity to Bristol through the African slave trade'.

This plaque was unveiled in 1997 during the European Year Against Racism by Ian White, at the time Member of the European Parliament for the Bristol constituency, and Philippa Gregory, whose novel *A Respectable Trade* is based on the slave trade and is set in Bristol. It is mounted on the side of a former quayside storage shed nearest Prince Street Bridge.

The
CLIFTON
Sausage®
· EST.2002 ·
BRISTOL

The Clifton Sausage Bar & Restaurant

This family run bar & restaurant offers the very best in British cooking. As their name suggests their speciality is sausages and they offer a wide range of delicious locally produced sausages, including Gloucester Old Spot pork, lamb, mint & apricot and beef and Butcombe ale.

The Clifton Sausage is more than a one trick pony; their menu also showcases a range of classic British dishes like starters of Cornish smoked haddock fishcakes, Old Spot pork cheek croquettes and goats curd, beetroot & watercress salad. Their hearty mains courses include 28 day aged 8oz Wiltshire rib-eye steak, shoulder of Wiltshire lamb, homemade burgers and wild mushroom & Bath blue cheese pie and are sure to satisfy even the hungriest of bellies. If your mouth isn't already salivating then The Clifton Sausages famous sticky toffee pudding, served with butterscotch sauce & vanilla ice cream is sure to tip you over the edge. It's been on their menu for over a decade is still their most popular pudding.

As well as the la carte main there is also a lunch menu, set party menu and a children's menu available. Their Sunday lunch menu offers one of the best roasts in all of Bristol and always features fabulous roast beef and Yorkshire puddings.

Set in the heart of beautiful Clifton village this charming independent restaurant is a firm favourite amongst both locals and visitors to the city.

The Clifton Sausage, 7-9 Portland Street, Clifton, Bristol, BS8 4JA

0117 973 1192

www.cliftonsausage.co.uk

info@cliftonsausage.co.uk

Also from The History Press